Storyology: Essays in Sea-Lore, and Plant-Lore

Benjamin Taylor

Alpha Editions

This edition published in 2024

ISBN : 9789362991942

Design and Setting By
Alpha Editions
www.alphaedis.com
Email - info@alphaedis.com

As per information held with us this book is in Public Domain.
This book is a reproduction of an important historical work. Alpha Editions uses the best technology to reproduce historical work in the same manner it was first published to preserve its original nature. Any marks or number seen are left intentionally to preserve its true form.

Contents

PREFACE. .... - 1 -

CHAPTER I. .... - 2 -

CHAPTER II. .... - 14 -

CHAPTER III. .... - 24 -

CHAPTER IV. .... - 34 -

CHAPTER V. .... - 45 -

CHAPTER VI. .... - 52 -

CHAPTER VII. .... - 60 -

CHAPTER VIII. .... - 66 -

CHAPTER IX. .... - 71 -

CHAPTER X. .... - 80 -

CHAPTER XI. .... - 88 -

CHAPTER XII. .... - 96 -

CHAPTER XIII. .... - 104 -

CHAPTER XIV. .... - 111 -

PREFACE.

THE principal object of this Foreword is to inform the expert Folkloreist and the case-hardened Mythologist (comparative or otherwise) that the following pages are intended for those who, being neither expert nor case-hardened, come under that gracious and catholic term—general reader. The writer addresses not the scholiast, but the ordinary person who likes to read about what he has not time to study.

Some portion of what is here printed has appeared in a once popular magazine now defunct. The author hastens to add, for the relief of the irreverent, that the journal long survived the ordeal of the publication. Nevertheless this book appears on its merits, or otherwise, and seeks no support from past attainment. Neither does it make any pretension to originality of matter or method, though it may, perhaps, contain one or two new ideas.

It is unnecessary to add that the publication is made only at the tearful entreaty of multitudinous friends. That, of course, is well understood among myth-hunters.

CHAPTER I.

STORYOLOGY.

I.

WHAT is a myth?

According to Webster, it is 'a fabulous or imaginary statement or narrative conveying an important truth, generally of a moral or religious nature: an allegory, religious or historical, of spontaneous growth and popular origin, generally involving some supernatural or superhuman claim or power; a tale of some extraordinary personage or country that has been gradually formed by, or has grown out of, the admiration and veneration of successive generations.' Here is a choice of three definitions, but not one of them is by itself satisfying. Let us rather say that a myth is a tradition in narrative form, more or less current in more or less differing garb among different races, to which religious or superhuman significations may be ascribable. We say 'may be' ascribable because, although the science of comparative mythology always seeks for such significations, it is probable that the modern interpretations are often as different from the original meaning as certain abstruse 'readings' of Shakespeare are from the poet's own thoughts.

In their introduction to Tales of the Teutonic Lands, Cox and Jones declare that the whole series of Arthurian legends are pure myths. These tales, they say, can be 'traced back to their earliest forms in phrases which spoke not of men and women, but of the Dawn which drives her white herds to their pastures'—the white clouds being the guardians of the cattle of the Sun—'of the Sun which slays the dew whom he loves, of the fiery dragon which steals the cattle of the lord of light, or the Moon which wanders with her myriad children through the heaven.' It is claimed that 'a strict etymological connection has been established' with regard to a large number of these and similar stories, 'but the link which binds the myth of the Hellenic Hephaistos with that of the Vedic Agni justifies the inference that both these myths reappear in those of Regin and of Wayland, or, in other words, that the story of the Dame of the Fine Green Kirtle is the story of Medeia, and that the tale of Helen is the legend of the loves of Conall Gulban. Elsewhere one reads that in the myth of Endymion, the Sun who has sunk to his dreamless sleep, the Moon appears as Asterodia journeying with her fifty daughters through the sky. 'In the Christian myth she becomes St. Ursula with her eleven thousand virgins—this Ursula again appearing in the myth of Tannhäuser, as the occupant of the Horselberg, and as the fairy queen in the tale of True Thomas of Ercildoune.' By the same method of comparative mythology, the whole series of the Arthurian stories are placed 'in that large family of heroic legends which have their origin in mythical phrases describing the phenomena of the outward world, and more especially those of the day and of the year.'

This seems hard, for it compels us to believe that our remote ancestors were very much more intelligent, and imaginative, and poetical, and religious than anything else which they have sent down to us would have suggested. It is true that Cox and Jones do not deny that the names which figure in many of these legends, as in those of Greece, may have been the names of real personages, but yet the narrative, they say, must not be taken as historical. This may be true, but in what sense can we regard it as more probable that the story-makers invented allegories, and clothed them with the names of contemporary or preceding heroes, than that they invented tales of wonder to fit these heroes? Is it easier to believe, for instance, that Arthur came after the myths, and was tacked on to them, than that the myths, or stories, came after Arthur, and were tacked on to him? Is there anything in the story of St. Ursula and her virgins which could not have had natural 'spontaneous growth' in an age of deep devotional faith in miracles, that we must be compelled to regard it as purely a mediævalized version of the Greek myth of the sun and moon?

I am not writing for experts and scholars, and therefore do not use the scientific terms and allusions familiar to students of these matters. I am merely writing for ordinary persons, who are often puzzled and pained by the extraordinary meanings which specialists contrive to twist out of simple and familiar things. It is not too much to say that the professional mythologists are among the most troublesome meddlers who disturb the repose of '*the average reader.*' Even Mr. Ruskin suffers in this connection. In The Queen of the Air he has given us one of his most delightful books, but there are probably few, outside the circle of philologists and comparative mythologists, who have not thought in reading the lovely interpretations of the myths of Athena, that there was more of Ruskin than of the Ancient Greek in the meaning evolved. Somehow, it seems easier to think that these things were conceived by a Professor of Art in the nineteenth century, than that they were the deliberate convictions of a primitive people ever so many centuries before Christ—a people, too, known to be steeped in sensualities, and addicted to very barbarous practices.

Are there, then, reasons for supposing that comparative mythologists are not always right—that, in fact, their science is but a doubtful science after all? Mr. Andrew Lang boldly says that there are. In Custom and Myth his object is to show the connection between savage customs—or rather the customs of savage and uncivilized races—and ancient myths. But before this branch of Storyology is reached, we must consider the question of the relation between our familiar nursery-tales, the folk-lore of our own and other countries, and the old romances, with these same myths. There is something more than monotony in the theory which 'resolves most of our old romances into a series of remarks about the weather.' The author of Primitive Culture (Mr. Tylor) rebels against this theory. There is no legend, no allegory, no nursery-rhyme, he says, safe from it, and, as an amusing illustration, he supposes the Song of Sixpence to be thus interpreted by the mythologists. Obviously, the four-and-twenty blackbirds are four-and-twenty hours, and the pie to hold them is the underlying earth covered with the over-arching sky. How true a touch of nature is it, 'when the pie is opened,' that is, when day breaks, 'the birds begin to sing!' The King is the Sun, and his 'counting out his money' is pouring out the sunshine, the golden shower of Danae; the Queen is the Moon, and her transparent honey the moonlight. The maid is the rosy-fingered Dawn, who rises before the Sun, her master, and hangs out the clothes (the clouds) across the sky; the particular blackbird who so tragically ends the tale, by 'nipping off her nose,' is the hour of sunrise. The time-honoured rhyme really wants, as Mr. Tylor remarks, only one thing to prove it a sun-myth, and that one thing is some other proof than a mere argument from analogy.

The same proof is wanting for those who would argue that the story of Red Riding Hood is only another dawn-myth. Mr. Hussin holds this view, but is not the story of the Cat and the Well capable of the same kind of reading? Pussy is the earth; Tommy, who shoves her into the well, is the evening or twilight; the well is Night; Johnny Stout is the Dawn who pulls the earth out of darkness again. There is no limit to this kind of application of so elastic a theory. But the very ease with which such explanations can be attached to any nursery-rhyme or folk-tale should warn us against their probability. As Mr. Tylor says: 'Rash inferences which, on the strength of mere resemblances, derive episodes of myth from episodes of nature, must be regarded with utter distrust, for the student who has no more stringent criterion than this for his myths of sun, and sky, and dawn, will find them wherever it pleases him to seek them.'

The mention of the story of Red Riding Hood suggests a familiar folk-tale, upon which that of Red Riding Hood may or may not have been founded, but which certainly forms the basis of a good many similar tales, and has been the subject of a good deal of wise exposition by the mythologists. In the story of the Wolf and the Seven Little Kids, as told by Grimm, there is a goat who goes out one day, leaving her seven little ones safely locked in the house, after warning them to beware of the wolf, whom she describes. The wolf comes begging for entrance, pretending to be their mother, but they distrust first his voice and then his black paws. He gets his paws whitened and comes back, showing them against the window as proof that he is indeed their mother. Therefore they open the door, and he swallows six of them, one after the other, without going through the ceremony of mastication. After this he goes back to the wood and falls asleep under a tree, where the disconsolate mother finds him. With the assistance of the seventh and youngest kid, who had escaped by hiding herself in the clock-case, the wolf is cut open, and the six kids jump out all alive and kicking. Stones are then placed in the wolf's stomach, and it is sewed up. When the wolf wakens he cannot account for the jumbling and tumbling in his stomach, so he goes to the well to get a drink. But the weight of the stones makes him top-heavy; he falls in and is drowned.

Now, there is nothing more remarkable in this story than there is in scores of our nursery or household tales, in which not only animals but also inanimate objects are gifted with speech, and in which the love of the marvellous rises superior to natural laws.

According to Cox, we must understand the myth of the Wolf and Kids thus: 'The wolf is here the night, or the darkness, which tries to swallow up the seven days of the week, and actually swallows six. The seventh—the youngest—escapes by hiding herself in the clock-case; in other words, the week is not quite run out, and before it comes to an end, the mother of the goats unrips the wolf's stomach and places stones in it in place of the little goats, who come trooping out, as the days of the week begin again to run their course.'

Very plausible this, from a comparative mythologist's point of view, and not easy to dispute—until we find that a similar tale is current all over the world where clock-cases are even yet unknown. We are told that the negroes of Georgia have such a legend; that the natives of Australia have one; that the Zulus have it; that the Indians of North America and of British Guiana, and the Malays, all have versions of it. In Brittany it is traceable in the legend of Gargantua; in Germany there are several variations; and in Greece it finds its counterpart in the legend of Saturn or Cronus. The Kaffirs tell the same story of a cannibal, but the way the negroes have it is like this: 'Old Mrs. Sow had five little pigs, whom she warned against the machinations of Brer Wolf. Old Mrs. Sow died, and each little pig built a house for himself. The youngest pig built the strongest house. Brer Wolf, by a series of stratagems, entrapped and devoured the four elder pigs. The youngest pig was the wisest, and would not let Brer Wolf come in by the door. He had to enter by way of the chimney, fell into a great fire the youngest pig had lighted, and was burned to death.' Here we have no clock-case, and no resurrection of the victims, but otherwise the *motif* of the story is the same. Certainly the negroes did not receive this tale from the white races, and it seems equally certain that they had no notion of typifying the dawn or the night, or anything else, but only the popular notion among nearly all primitive peoples that the youngest is usually the most specially gifted and blessed.

This is Mr. Lang's view: 'In the tale of the Wolf and the Seven Kids, the essence is found in the tricks whereby the wolf deceives his victims; in the victory of the goat; in the disgorging of the kids alive; and the punishment of the wolf (as of Cronus in Hesiod) by the stone which he is obliged to admit into his system. In these events there is nothing allegorical or mystical, no reference to sunrise or storms. The crude ideas and incidents are of world-wide range, and suit the fancy of the most backward nation.' The only thing in Grimm's tale which differs materially from those of 'world-wide range' is the clock-case—clearly a modern addition, but an item which forms an essential factor in Cox's definition of the 'myth.'

So much by way of illustration; but dozens of tales might be produced, all pointing the same way. This is to the belief that, although stories have unquestionably been transmitted from race to race throughout the ages, and so have become widely distributed over the world, all the current nursery, or household, or folk, stories have not necessarily been so transmitted from some one creative race of myth-makers. We have just seen how an evidently modern interpolation (a clock-case) has come to be regarded as an essential part of a myth, and it is surely easier to believe that the other features are relics of some ancient customs of which we have no record, than that they bear the ingenious references to natural phenomena which the mythologists suppose.

Max Müller holds that all the stories of princesses, imprisoned or enchanted, and delivered by young lovers, 'can be traced back to mythological tradition about the Spring being released from the bonds of Winter.' But he requires, first, to have the names of the personages of the story, because he traces the connection more by their etymology than by the incidents of the narrative—of which more anon. With regard to purely nursery or household tales, the question seems to resolve itself pretty much into this: Are they the remains of an older and higher mythology, or are they the foundations upon which the priests and medicine-men and minstrels of later ages built their myths? Are they, in short, surviving relics, or were they germs? The favourite scientific theory adopts the former view; I incline to the latter. There are many of the familiar folk-tales which it is impossible to explain, and there are many, doubtless, which are in some sort fragments of the old mythologies filtered to us through Greece. But, on the whole, it is more reasonable to conclude that the simple stories of the marvellous or irrational have their origin in 'the qualities of the uncivilized imagination.'

Thus, with regard to the current superstitions of our peasantry and of the Highlanders, it is much more rational to consider them, as Dr. Robert Chambers did, as 'springing from a disposition of the human mind to account for actual appearances by some imagined history which the appearances suggest,' than as relics of the old-world mythologies. The untutored mind disregards the natural, even in these days of applied science. There is an old weir across the Tweed which the common people, forgetting the mill, that had disappeared, pointed out as the work of one of the imps of Michael Scott, the wizard. Wherever there are three-topped hills there is sure to be a legend of the work of this same Michael, or some other wizard. In the same way, deep, clear lakes exist in various parts of the country, concerning which traditions survive of cities lying at the bottom, submerged for their wickedness, or by the machinations of some evil spirit. Old buildings exist in many parts in such unfavourable situations that popular tradition can only account for the singularity by the operation of some unfriendly spirit transporting them from their original locality. Large solitary rocks off the coast, or on hilltops, have been deposited where they are by witches. Water springing from a rock by the roadside has always been the result of the stroke of some magician or saint. Large depressions on hillsides are generally the footprints of giants, like the mark left by Buddha's foot as he ascended to heaven, still to be seen on a hill in Ceylon. The circular green marks in the fields are the rings drawn by the fairies for their midnight dances, and a scaur or cliff bearing the marks of volcanic action or of lightning is invariably associated with some tale of diabolic fury. Almost every reader can add instances of natural appearances or effects idealized by the workings of the imagination of uncivilized or uncultivated minds.

II.

One of the most common forms of these idealized phenomena is that known as the 'Fairy-ring,' about which Nether Lochaber has said, in the Highlands of Scotland, 'We can perfectly understand how in the good old times, ere yet the schoolmaster was abroad, or science had become a popular plaything, people—and doubtless very honest, decent people, too—attributed those inexplicable emerald circles to supernatural agency; if, indeed, anything connected with the "good folks" or "men of peace" could properly be called supernatural in times when a belief in fairies and every sort of fairy freak and frolic was deemed the most correct and natural thing in the world. Did not these circles, it was argued, appear in the course of a single night? In the sequestered woodland glade, nor herd nor milkmaid could see anything odd or unusual as the sun went down, and lo! next morning, as they drove their flocks afield, there was the mysterious circle, round as the halo about the wintry moon.... And if we know better nowadays than to believe these green circles to be fairy-rings, we also know better than to give the slightest credence to certain authors of our own day who have gravely asserted that they are caused by electricity.... Fairy-rings ... are in truth caused by a mushroom (*Agaricus pratensis*), the sporule dust or seed of which, having fallen on a spot suitable for its growth, instantly germinates, and, constantly propagating itself by sending out a network of innumerable filaments and threads, forms the rich green rings so common everywhere.'

Hardly more excusable than the electricity theorists, thinks this writer, are those learned authors who tell us that the West received the first hint of the existence of fairies from the East at the time of the Crusades, and that almost all our fairy lore is traceable to the same source, 'the fact being that Celt and Saxon, Scandinavian and Goth, Lapp and Finn, had their "dûergar," their "elfen" without number, such as dun-elfen, berg-elfen, munt-elfen, feld-elfen, sae-elfen and waeter-elfen—elves or spirits of downs, hills and mountains, of the fields, of the woods, of the sea, and of the rivers, streams and solitary pools—fairies, in short, and a complete fairy mythology, long centuries before Peter the Hermit was born, or Frank and Moslem dreamt of making the Holy Sepulchre a *casus belli*.'

There is something very suggestive in these remarks, and one thought suggested is particularly in the direction of our inquiry, and that is, may not the theory of the Aryan mythological origin of our folk-tales be as imaginary and as groundless as the theory of the Oriental origin of fairies? At the same time, let us admit that the superstitious belief in capnomancy—*i.e.*, divination by smoke—still said to be prevalent in some parts of the Highlands, is probably the relic of the old sacrifices by fire to the gods. In so far the superstition has a mythological significance, but then, are we not driven back to the consideration whether these gods were not actual personages in the minds of the old Celtic worshippers, and not symbols of natural phenomena?

So much, however, for popular superstitions; and, as regards folk-tales, we must, in speculating as to their origin,[1] 'look not into the clouds, but upon the earth; not in the various aspects of nature, but in the daily occurrences and surroundings.' The process of diffusion must always remain uncertain. 'Much may be due to the identity everywhere of early fancy, something to transmission,' but 'household tales occupy a middle place between the stories of savages and the myths of early civilization.'[2] And as nursery-rhymes are but the simplified form of household or folk-tales, let us consider with Mr. Lang the relation between savage customs and ancient myths.

The foundation of the method of comparative mythology is the belief that 'myths are the result of a disease of language, as the pearl is the result of a disease of the oyster.' The method of inquiry is to examine the names which occur in the stories, and having found or invented a meaning for these names, to argue back from them to a meaning in the myths. But then almost each scholar has his peculiar fancy in etymology, and while one finds a Sanskrit root, another finds a Greek, a third a Semitic, and so on. Even when they agree upon the derivation of the proper names, the scholars seldom agree upon the interpretation of them, and thus the whole system is full of perplexity and confusion to all who approach its study with unbiassed minds. There is a further division among the mythologists, for there are some who have a partiality for sun-myths, others for cloud-myths, sky-myths and fire-myths, and each seeks to work out an interpretation of an old-world story to suit his own taste in myths. How can they be all right? And in whom can we have confidence when we find so much disagreement, first, on the derivation of names, and second, on their meaning after the derivation is discovered? And then, how do we know that words had the same meaning to the ancients as they have to us? Was the sky, for instance, to the original story-makers 'an airy, infinite, radiant vault,' as it is to us, or was it a material roof, or even a person? And, further, how is it that we find the same myth, with slight alterations, in various parts of the world, but with totally different names?

In opposition to the method of reading myths by the philological analysis of names, there is the method of reading them by folk-lore, *i.e.*, by a comparison of the folk-tales and customs of primitive peoples. The student of folk-lore has to collect and compare the similar relics of old races, the surviving superstitions and traditions, and the ideas which still live. He is thus led to compare the usages, myths, and ideas of savages with those which remain among the European peasantry—classes which have least altered by education, and have shown the smallest change in progress. It is thus that we find even in our own country and in our own day such things as the beliefs in fairies and divination by smoke, which are as old as time. Similarly, the harvest-custom which is still practised by the children in parts of rural England and Scotland—the dressing up of the last gleaning in human shape, and conducting it home in musical procession—is parallel with a custom in ancient Peru, and with the Feast of Demeter of the Sicilians. But that does not necessarily prove any original connection between Peruvians, Scotch and Sicilians, any more than the fact that the negroes of Barbadoes make clay figures of their enemies and mutilate them, as the Greeks and Accadians of old used to do, proves any connection between the negroes and the Greeks and Accadians. If we find the Australians spreading dust round the body of a dead man in order to receive the impression of the footprints of any ghostly visitor, the same custom has been observed among the Jews, among the Aztecs, among the French, and even among the Scotch. Where we find, therefore, an apparently irrational and anomalous custom in any country, we must look for a country where a similar custom prevails, and where it is no longer irrational and anomalous, but in harmony with the manners and ideas of the people among whom it prevails. When we read of Greeks dancing about in their 'mysteries' with live serpents, it seems unintelligible, but when we read of Red Indians doing the same thing with live rattlesnakes, we can understand the meaning because we can see implied a test of physical courage. May not a similar motive have originated the Greek practices?

The method of folk-lore, then, is 'to compare the seemingly meaningless customs or manners of civilized races with the similar customs and manners which exist among the uncivilized, and still retain their meaning. It is not necessary for comparison of this sort that the uncivilized and the civilized race should be of the same stock, nor need we prove that they were ever in contact.'[3] Similar conditions of mind produce similar practices, apart from identity of race, or borrowing of ideas and manners. In pursuing this method we have to compare the customs and tales of the most widely separated races, whereas the comparative mythologists, who hold it correct to compare Greek, Slavonic, Celtic and Indian stories because they occur in languages of the same family, and Chaldean and Greek stories because the Chaldeans and the Greeks are known to have been in contact, will not compare Greek, Chaldean, Celtic, or Indian stories with those of the Maoris, the Eskimos, or the Hottentots, because these last belong to a different language-family, and are not known to have ever been in contact with Aryan races.

The 'bull-roarer,' a toy familiar to most children, is one example selected by Mr. Lang. It is a long, thin, narrow piece of wood, sharpened at both ends; attached to a piece of string, and whirled rapidly and steadily in the air, it emits a sound which gradually increases to an unearthly kind of roar. The ancient Greeks employed at some of their sacred rites a precisely similar toy, described by historians as 'a little piece of wood, to which a string was fastened, and in the mysteries it is whirled round to make a roaring noise.' The performers in the 'mysteries' at which this implement was used daubed themselves all over with clay. Demosthenes describes the mother of Æschines as a dabbler in mysteries, and tells how Æschines used to assist her by helping to bedaub the initiate with clay and bran. Various explanations have been offered of these practices, but let us see how they tally with any prevailing customs. First, the bull-roarer is to be found in almost every country in the world, and among the most primitive peoples. It is so simple an instrument that it is within the scope of the mechanical genius of the most degraded savages, and therefore it is quite unnecessary to suppose that the idea of it was ever transmitted from race to race. And as an instrument employed in religious rites or mysteries, it is found in New Mexico, in Australia, in New Zealand and in Africa, to this day. Its use in Australia is to warn the women to keep out of the way when the men are about to celebrate their tribal mysteries. It is death for women to witness these rites, and it is also forbidden for them to look upon the sacred turndun, or bull-roarer. In the same way, among the Greeks, it was forbidden for men to witness the rites of the women, and for women to witness those of the men. Among the Indians of Zuni, Mr. Cushing found the same implement used by the priests to summon the tribe to the sacrificial feasts. In South Africa, Mr. Tylor has proved that the bull-roarer is employed to call the men only to the celebration of sacred functions, and the instrument itself is described in Theal's Kaffir Folklore.

Now, the same peoples who still employ the bull-roarer as a sacred instrument also bedaub their bodies with clay, for no apparent reason unless it may be to frighten their enemies or repel intruders. We thus find still prevailing in our own time among savage races practices which are perfectly analogous to practices which prevailed among the Greeks. The reasonable inference, therefore, is not that the bull-roaring and body-daubing were first used in the rites of a civilized race of Greeks, and thence transmitted to Africa, Australia and America, but that the employment of these things by the Greeks was a survival of the time when the Greeks were in the same savage condition as are the peoples among whom we find the same things now.

The Greek story of Saturn is familiar to every schoolboy. Saturn, it will be remembered, wounds and drives away his father, Uranus, because of his unkindness to himself and his brothers. Afterwards Saturn marries his sister Rhea, and has several children—Demeter, Hera, Hades, Poseidon and Zeus—whom he swallowed as they were born, lest they might serve him as he served Uranus. But Rhea didn't like this, and at the time when Zeus was born she ran away to a distant place. Saturn followed, and, asking for the child, was given a stone, which he swallowed without looking at it. Zeus grew up in security, and in due time gave his father a dose which made him disgorge, first, the stone (which was placed at Delphi, where it became an object of public worship), and then the children, one after another, all living and hearty.

The tale is told in various ways, but these are the main incidents. It is interpreted by the mythologists to typify, in its first part, the birth of the world and the elements; and the second part is held by some to typify the operations of time, by others the alternations of night and day—the stone swallowed by Saturn being the sun, which he afterwards disgorges at daybreak. By others Saturn is held to be the sun and ripener of the harvests; by others, again, the storm-god, who swallows the clouds, whose sickle is the rainbow, and whose blood is the lightning; by others still Saturn is regarded as the sky, which swallows and reproduces the stars, and whose sickle is the crescent moon. There is a great deal of diversity of opinion, it will be observed, about this myth of Saturn, or Cronus, but it is curious to note how all the leading incidents of this myth may be traced in various parts of the world.[4] Among the Maoris, the story of Tûtenganahaû is told, and this is a story of the severing of heaven and earth, very similar to the Greek story. In India and in China, legends tell of the former union of heaven and earth, and of their violent separation by their own children. As regards the swallowing performances of Saturn, they find analogues in tales among the Australians, among the Red Indians, among the natives of British Guiana, and among the Kaffirs.

The conclusion, then, is that the first part of the Saturn myth is evidently the survival of an old nature-myth which is common to races who never had any communication with the Greeks. The second part is unintelligible, except as just such a legend as might be evolved by persons in the same savage intellectual condition as, say, the Bushmen, who account for celestial phenomena by saying that a big star has swallowed his daughter and spat her out again.

Any myth which accounts for the processes of nature or the aspects of natural phenomena may, says Mr. Lang, conceivably have been invented separately, therefore it is not surprising to find the star-stories of savages closely resembling those of civilized races. The story of the lost sister of the Pleiades, according to the Greek myth, finds a parallel in a tradition among the Australians. Of star-lore generally, it may be said that it is much the same even among the Bushmen of Africa, as it was among the Greeks and Egyptians, and as it is among the Australians and Eskimos.

Another interesting inquiry is to trace the legend current among the Greeks, and known to us as that of Jason and the Golden Fleece, in the Storyology of the Africans, the Norse, the Malagasies, the Russians, the Italians, the Samoans, the Finns, the Samoyedes and the Eskimo. Some of the resemblances are so exceedingly close and curious as to severely shake our belief in the dawn-sun-spring-lightning interpretations of the mythologists. They drive us to the conclusion that the Jason myth is not a story capable of explanation as a nature-myth, or as a result of 'a disease of language'; for as is pertinently remarked, 'So many languages could not take the same malady in the same way; nor can we imagine any stories of natural phenomena that would inevitably suggest this tale to so many diverse races.'

The rational theory is that the Jason story, like its analogues among strange races, had its origin in a time of savage conditions, when animals were believed to talk, when human sacrifices and cannibalism were practised, and when efforts to escape being eaten were natural.

CHAPTER II.

THE MAGIC WAND.

IT is sufficiently remarkable that the rod, besides being an emblem of authority, is also an instrument of the supernatural. An indispensable instrument, one may say; for was ever a magician depicted in book, in picture, or in the mind's eye, without a wand? Does even the most amateurish of prestidigitateurs attempt to emulate the performances of the once famous Wizard of the North, without the aid of the magic staff? The magician, necromancer, soothsayer, or conjurer, is as useless without his wand as a Newcastle pitman is without his 'daug.'

At first thought it might be assumed that the association of the rod or wand with necromancy is merely an indication of power or authority, in the same way as the sceptre is associated with kingship. But there is something more in it. Magic has been well called 'the shadow of religion,' and the early religious idea found expression in symbols. These symbols, as we know, have in many cases retained a certain significance long after the ideas they were meant to convey have been lost, or abandoned, or modified. If we bear these things in mind, it is not difficult to discover a religious origin for the symbolic wand of necromancy.

Mr. Moncure Conway, in his book on Demonology and Devil-lore, mentions a thing which seems peculiarly apposite to our subject. In the old town of Hanover there is a certain schoolhouse, in which, above the teacher's chair, there was originally a representation of a dove perched upon a rod—the rod in this case being meant to typify a branch. Below the dove and rod there was this inscription: 'This shall lead you unto all Truth.' But the dove has long since disappeared, and there remains now but the rod and the inscription. It is natural that the children of the school should apply the admonition to the rod, ignorant that the rod was but the supporter of a symbol of the Holy Spirit. Thus has the pious design of inculcating a Divine lesson left only an emblem of mysterious terror. In some way, too, has the magic wand lost its religious significance and become but a dread implement of the occult.

Yet we might trace the origin of the magician's wand to the very same root as that of the iron rod of the Hanover schoolhouse. We may find it in the olive-branch brought by the dove into the ark—a message of Divine love and mercy—and therefore a connecting-link between human needs and desires and superhuman power. To construe a mere symbol into a realized embodiment of the virtue symbolized were surely as easy in this case as in that of the Eucharist.

But if this suggestion of the origin of the magician's wand be thought too hypothetical, there will be less objection to our finding it in Aaron's rod. Moses was commanded to take a rod from the chiefs of each of the twelve tribes, and to write upon each rod the name. The rods were then to be placed in the Tabernacle, and the owner of the one which blossomed was designated as the chosen one. The rod of the house of Levi bore the name of Aaron, and this was the only one of the twelve which blossomed. Here once more was the rod used to connect human needs with Divine will; but now a special virtue is made to appear in the rod itself. This virtue appeared again, when Pharaoh called all the sorcerers and magicians of Egypt to test their enchantments with Aaron's. All these magicians bore wands, or rods, and when they threw them on the ground the rods turned into serpents. Aaron's rod also turned into a serpent, and swallowed all the others. Now, here we find two things established. First, that even in these early days necromancy was a profession, and the rod a necessary implement of the craft; and, second, that the rod was esteemed not merely an emblem of authority, or a mere ornament of office, but as a thing of superhuman power in itself although the power could only be evoked by the specially gifted.

We find the beginning of the idea in the story of Moses' rod which turned into a serpent when he cast it on the ground at the Divine command. This was what led up to the trial of skill with the Egyptian magicians, and seems to have been the first suggestion in early history of the miraculous virtues of the rod. Then we must remember that it was by the stretching forth of the rod of the prophet that all the waters of Egypt were made to turn into blood, and that the plagues of frogs and lice were wrought, and that the hail was called down from heaven which destroyed the crops and flocks of the Egyptians. In fact, all the miracles performed in the land of Egypt were made to appear more or less as the result of the application of the magic rod, just as to this day the clever conjurer appears to produce his wonderful effects with his wand.

It was by the stretching forth of the rod of Moses that the Red Sea divided, and that the water sprang from the rock. The staff of Elisha and the spear of Joshua may also be cited in this connection, and other examples in Holy Writ may occur to the reader. They are mentioned here in no spirit of irreverence, but merely as evidence that the magic virtue of the rod was a fixed belief in the minds of the early writers.

Belief in the vitalizing power of the rod may be found embalmed in many a curious mediæval legend. The budding rod, borrowed from the tradition of

Aaron's, is, for instance, very frequent. Thus in the story of St. Christophoros, as preserved in Von Bülow's Christian Legends of Germany, we read of the godly man carrying the Child-Christ on his back through a raging torrent, and afterwards lying down on the banks of the stream, exhausted, to sleep. The staff which he stuck in the ground ere he lay down, budded and blossomed before he awoke, and in the morning he found a great umbrageous tree bearing fruit, and giving shelter to hundreds of gorgeous birds. There are many such legends in the traditions of all the Christian nations, and the collection and comparison of them would be an interesting and instructive task, but one too large for our present purpose.

It is related by Holinshed, in connection with many wonderful visions which were seen in Scotland about A.D. 697, that once when the Bishop was conducting the service in the church of Camelon, with the crozier-staff in his hand, 'it was kindled so with fire that by no means it could be quenched till it was burnt even to ashes.' This was supposed to have been the handiwork of the devil, who has on other occasions used the staff or wand to emphasize his intentions or mark his spite. Thus, of the famous Dr. Fian it is narrated in the 'Newes from Scotland, declaring the damnable Life of Doctor Fian, a notable Sorcerer, who was burned at Edenborough in Januarie last 1591; which Doctor was Register to the Devill, that sundrie times Preached at North-Baricke Kirke to a number of notorious Witches,' etc.—that he made the following, among his other confessions: 'That the devill had appeared unto him in the night before, appareled all in blacke, with a white wand in his hande, and that the devill demanded of him if he would continue his faithfull service according to his first oath and promise made to that effect, whome (as hee then said) he utterly renounced to his face, and said unto him in this manner: "Avoide, avoide, Satan, for I have listened too much unto thee, and by the same thou hast undone me, in respect whereof I utterly forsake thee." To whom the devill answered, "That once, ere thou die, thou shalt be mine," and with that (as he sayed) the devill brake the white wand, and immediately vanished from sight.' After which, the chronicle goes on to tell how the redoubtable doctor actually escaped from prison, and began to resume his Satanic practices.

This brings us to the most frequent use of the rod in superstitions—for the purposes of divination. There is a suggestion of the practice by Nebuchadnezzar, when he 'stood at the parting of the way, at the head of two ways, to use divinations, he made his arrows bright,' etc. He then threw up a bundle of arrows to see which way they would alight, and because they fell on the right hand he marched towards Jerusalem. Divination by the wand is also suggested in the shooting of an arrow from a window by Elisha, and by the strokes upon the ground with an arrow by which Joash foretold the number of his victories.

Sir Thomas Browne speaks of a common 'practice among us to determine doubtful matters by the opening of a book and letting fall of a staff.' The 'staff' business is not quite so familiar in present days, but the opening of a book for prophetic guidance is, perhaps, more common than most people suppose.

Sir Thomas Browne also speaks of a 'strange kind of exploration and peculiar way of Rhabdomancy' used in mineral discoveries. That is, 'with a fork of hazel, commonly called Moses his rod, which, freely held forth, will stir and play if any mine be under it. And though many there are,' says the learned doctor, 'who have attempted to make it good, yet until better information, we are of opinion, with Agricola, that in itself it is a fruitless exploration, strongly scenting of pagan derivation and the *virgula divina* proverbially magnified of old. The ground whereof were the magical rods in poets—that of Pallas, in Homer; that of Mercury, that charmed Argus; and that of Circe, which transformed the followers of Ulysses. Too boldly usurping the name of Moses' rod, from which notwithstanding, and that of Aaron, were probably occasioned the fables of all the rest. For that of Moses must needs be famous unto the Egyptians, and that of Aaron unto many other nations, as being preserved in the Ark until the destruction of the Temple built by Solomon.'

One may look in vain, perhaps, for modern instances of the divining-rod under the name of 'Moses his rod,' as old Sir Thomas found it.

It is curious, however, that Sir Thomas Browne, who was so fond of delving among ancient writers, makes no reference to a striking passage in Herodotus. That historian, speaking of the Scythians, says, 'They have amongst them a great number who practise the art of divination. For this purpose they use a number of willow-twigs in this manner: they bring large bundles of these together, and having untied them, dispose them one by one on the ground, each bundle at a distance from the rest. This done, they pretend to foretell the future, during which they take up the bundles separately and tie them again together.'

From this it may be seen that while the divining-rod was a familiar instrument 450 years before Christ, it was also then disbelieved in by some. Curious to think that what the old historian of Halicarnassus was wise enough to ridicule four centuries and a half before the birth of Christ, there are yet people, nineteen centuries after His advent, simple enough to accept!

Herodotus goes on to tell that this mode of divination was hereditary among the Scythians, so how many centuries earlier it may have been practised one can hardly guess. He says that the 'enaries, or effeminate men, affirm that the art of divination was taught them by the goddess Venus,' a statement which will carry some significance to those who are familiar with the theories so boldly advocated by the author of Bible Folklore.

Now, the attempt to divine by means of rods, arrows, staffs or twigs is evidently a good deal older than Herodotus, and it is to be found among almost every race of people on the face of the earth. Let us say 'almost,' because Mr. Andrew Lang instances this as one form of superstition which is not prevalent among savage races; or rather, to use his exact words, 'is singular in its comparative lack of copious savage analogues.' The qualification seems to be necessary, because there are certainly some, if not 'copious,' instances among savage peoples of the use of the divining-rod in one form or other. And Mr. Lang is hardly accurate in speaking of the 'resurrection' of this superstition in our own country. It has, in fact, never died, and there is scarcely a part of the country where a 'diviner' has not tried his—or her, for it is often a woman—skill with the 'twig' from time to time. These attempts have seldom been known beyond the immediate locality and the limited circle of those interested in them, and it is only of late years, since folklore became more of a scientific and general study, that the incidents have been seized upon and recorded by the curious. From the time of Moses until now the 'rod' has been almost continuously used by innumerable peoples in the effort to obtain supplies of water.

In ancient times it was used, as we have seen, for a variety of other purposes; but its surviving use in our generation is to indicate the locality of hidden springs or of mineral deposits. There are cases on record, however, so recently as the last century, when the rod was used in the detection of criminals, and a modified application of it to a variety of indefinite purposes may even be traced to the planchette, which, at this very day, is seriously believed in by many persons who are ranked as 'intelligent.'

Now, of the use of the divining-rod in England, Mr. Thiselton-Dyer thus wrote some years ago: 'The *virgula divinatoria*, or divining-rod, is a forked branch in the form of a Y, cut off a hazel-stick, by means of which people have pretended to discover mines, springs, etc., underground. It is much employed in our mining districts for the discovery of hidden treasure. In Cornwall, for instance, the miners place much confidence in its indications, and even educated, intelligent men oftentimes rely on its supposed virtues. Pryce, in his Mineralogia Cornubiensis, tells us that many mines have been discovered by the rod, and quotes several; but after a long account of the method of cutting, tying and using it, rejects it, because 'Cornwall is so plentifully stored with tin and copper lodes, that some accident every week discovers to us a fresh vein,' and because 'a grain of metal attracts the rod as strongly as a pound, for which reason it has been found to dip equally to a poor as to a rich lode.'

But in Lancashire and Cumberland also, Mr. Dyer goes on to say, 'the power of the divining-rod is much believed in, and also in other parts of England.' The method of using it is thus described. The small ends, being crooked, are to be held in the hands in a position flat or parallel to the horizon, and the upper part at an elevation having an angle to it of about seventy degrees. The rod must be grasped strongly and steadily, and then the operator walks over the ground. When he crosses a lode, its bending is supposed to indicate the presence thereof. Mr. Dyer's explanation of the result is simple: 'The position of the hands in holding the rod is a constrained one—it is not easy to describe it; but the result is that the hands, from weariness speedily induced in the muscles, grasp the end of the twig yet more rigidly, and thus is produced the mysterious bending. The phenomena of the divining-rod and table-turning are of precisely the same character, and both are referable to an involuntary muscular action resulting from fixedness of idea. These experiments with a divining-rod are always made in a district known to be metalliferous, and the chances are, therefore, greatly in favour of its bending over or near a mineral lode.'

The theory of 'involuntary muscular action' is a favourite explanation, and the subject is one well worthy of the investigation of all students of psychology. But how does this theory square with the story of Linnæus, told by a writer in *The Gentleman's Magazine* in 1752? 'When Linnæus was upon his voyage to Scania, hearing his secretary highly extol the virtues of his divining-rod, he was willing to convince him of its insufficiency, and for that purpose concealed a purse of 100 ducats under a ranunculus which grew up by itself in a meadow, and bid the secretary find it if he could. The wand discovered nothing, and Linnæus's mark was soon trampled down by the company who were present, so that when Linnæus went to finish the experiment by fetching the gold himself, he was utterly at a loss where to find it. The man with the wand assisted him, and told him that it could not lie in the way they were going, but quite the contrary; so pursued the direction of the wand, and actually dug out the gold. Linnæus adds, that such another experiment would be sufficient to make a proselyte of him.'

The explanation of this case by the incredulous would, of course, be that the owner of the wand had made a private mark of his own, and thus knew better than Linnæus where the gold lay.

The divining-rod, however, is not used only in districts which are known to abound in metalliferous deposits, when minerals are being searched for, but has frequently been used by prospectors in new countries. Thus we recall that Captains Burton and Cameron in their book about the Gold Coast, tell how the rod was used by the early British explorers on the Gambia River. One Richard Jobson, in 1620, landed and searched various parts of the country, armed with mercury, nitric acid, some large crucibles, and a divining-rod. He washed the sand and examined the rocks beyond the Falls of Barraconda, with small success for a long time. At last, however, he found what he declared to be 'the mouth of the mine itself, and found gold in such abundance as surprised him with joy and admiration.' But what part the divining-rod played in the discovery is not related, and, for the rest, 'the mine' has disappeared as mysteriously as it was discovered. No one else has seen it, and all the gold that now comes from the Gambia River is a small quantity of dust washed down from the mountain-ridges of the interior. It is curious, however, to find civilized Europeans carrying the divining-rod to one of the districts where, according to Mr. Andrew Lang, it has no analogue among the primitive savages.

I have mentioned, on the authority of Mr. Thiselton-Dyer, some of the districts of England in which the divining-rod is still more or less used. But something of its more extended use may be learned from Mr. Hilderic Friend's Flowers and Flower-Lore. That writer informs us of a curious custom of the hop-pickers of Kent and Sussex for ascertaining where they shall stand to pick. One of them cuts as many slips of hazel as there are bins in the garden, and on these he cuts notches from one upwards. Each picker then draws a twig, and his standing is decided by the number upon it. This is certainly an interesting instance of the divination by twigs reduced to practical ends. The same writer regards the familiar 'old-wife' fortune-telling by tea-leaves as merely another variation of this old superstition. It does seem to have some analogy to several of the practices to which we have briefly referred, and one finds another analogy in the Chinese custom of divining by straws.

The divining-rod of England is described by Mr. Friend much in the same way as by Mr. Dyer. But, according to Mr. Friend, hazel was not always, although it has for a long time been, the favourite wood for the purpose. Elder, at any rate, is strictly forbidden, as deemed incapable of exhibiting magical powers. In Wiltshire and elsewhere Mr. Friend knows of the magic rod having been used recently for detecting water. It must be cut at some particular time when the stars are favourable, and 'in cutting it, one must face the east, so that the rod shall be one which catches the first rays of the morning sun, or, as some say, the eastern and western sun must shine through the fork of the rod, otherwise it will be good for nothing.'

The same superstition prevails in China with regard to rods cut from the magic peach-tree. In Prussia, it is said, hazel-rods are cut in spring, and when harvest comes they are placed in crosses over the grain to keep it good for years, while in Bohemia the rod is used to cure fevers. A twig of apple-tree is, in some parts, considered as good as a hazel-rod, but it must be cut by the seventh son of a seventh son. Brand records that he has known ash-twigs used, and superstitiously regarded, in some parts of

England; but the hazel is more generally supposed to be popular with the fairies, or whoever may be the mysterious spirits who guide the diviner's art. Hence perhaps the name, common in some parts, of witch-hazel, although, of course, philologists will have it that the true derivation is wych. In Germany the witch-hazel is the *zauber-streuch*, or the magic-tree, and it is probable that both witch and wych are from the Anglo-Saxon *wic-en*, to bend. It is curious, at any rate, that while in olden times a witch was called *wicce*, the mountain-ash, which, as we have seen, has supposed occult virtues, was formerly called *wice*. Whether this root has any connection with another name by which the magic wand is known—viz., the wishing-rod—may be doubted, but there is clearly a close connection between the hazel-twig of superstitious England and the *Niebelungen-rod* of Germany, which gave to its possessor power over all the world.

Of the employment of the divining-rod for the detection of criminals there are many cases on record, but the most famous in comparatively recent times is that of Jacques Aymar of Lyons. The full details of the doings of this remarkable person are given by Mr. Baring-Gould in his Curious Myths of the Middle Ages; but the story is told more concisely by another writer: 'On July 5, 1692, a vintner and his wife were found dead in the cellar of their shop at Lyons. They had been killed by blows from a hedging-knife, and their money had been stolen. The culprits could not be discovered, and a neighbour took upon him to bring to Lyons a peasant out of Dauphiné, named Jacques Aymar, a man noted for his skill with the divining-rod. The Lieutenant-Criminel and the Procureur du Roi took Aymar into the cellar, furnishing him with a rod of the first wood that came to hand. According to the Procureur du Roi the rod did not move till Aymar reached the very spot where the crime had been committed. His pulse then beat, and the wand twisted rapidly. Guided by the wand, or by some internal sensation, Aymar now pursued the track of the assassins, entered the court of the Archbishop's palace, left the town by the bridge over the Rhone, and followed the right bank of the river. He reached a gardener's house, which he declared the men had entered, and some children confessed that three men, whom they described, had come into the house one Sunday morning. Aymar followed the track up the river, pointed out all the places where the men had landed, and, to make a long story short, stopped at last at the door of the prison of Beaucaire. He was admitted, looked at the prisoners, and picked out as the murderer a little hunchback, who had just been brought in for a small theft. The hunchback was taken to Lyons, and he was recognised on the way by the people at all the stages where he had stopped. At Lyons he was examined in the usual manner, and confessed that he had been an accomplice in the crime, and had guarded the door. Aymar pursued the other culprits to the coast, followed them by sea, landed where they had landed, and only desisted from his search when they crossed the frontier. As for the hunchback, he was broken on the wheel, being condemned on his own confession.'

This is briefly the story of Jacques Aymar, which is authenticated by various eye-witnesses, and of which many explanations have been tendered from time to time. Mr. Baring-Gould commits himself to no definite expression of opinion, but says: 'I believe that the imagination is the principal motive force in those who use the divining-rod; but whether it is so solely I am unable to decide. The powers of Nature are so mysterious and inscrutable that we must be cautious in limiting them, under abnormal conditions, to the ordinary laws of experience.' As, however, Jacques Aymar failed ignominiously under all the subsequent trials to which he was subjected, the most reasonable explanation of his success, with regard to the Lyons murder, is that he was by nature a clever detective, and that he was favoured by circumstances after he had once caught a clue.

To return to the employment of the divining-rod in England, we find numerous instances of its application in searching for water, and these instances happen to be among the best authenticated of any on record. Some years ago a writer in the *Times* boldly declared that he had himself seen the rod successfully used in seeking for water. He had even tried it himself, with the determination that the rod should not be allowed to twist, 'even if an ocean rolled under his feet.' But he confessed that it did twist in spite of him, and that at the place was found a concealed spring.

Then it is recorded of Lady Milbanke, mother of Lord Byron's wife, that she had found a well by the violent twisting of the twig held in the orthodox way in her hand—turning so violently, indeed, as almost to break her fingers. Dr. Hutton was a witness of the affair, and has recorded his experience, which is quoted in a curious book called Jacob's Rod, published in London many years ago. This case, and others, were cited by a writer in the twenty-second volume of the *Quarterly Review*. De Quincey also asserted that he had frequently seen the divining-rod successfully used in the quest of water, and declared that, 'whatever science or scepticism may say, most of the tea-kettles in the Vale of Wrington, North Somersetshire, are filled by Rabdomancy.' Mr. Baring-Gould also quotes the case of a friend of his own who was personally acquainted with a Scotch lady who could detect hidden springs with a twig, which was inactive in the hands of others who tried it on the same spots.

Other instances might be cited, but enough has been said to show that the magic rod, from the earliest periods, has been an instrument of supernatural attributes, and that even to this day in our own country it is still believed by some to have the special faculty of indicating the presence of minerals and water. With regard to minerals, there are no instances so well authenticated as those concerning the discovery of water. With regard to these last a considerable amount of haziness still exists, and, without venturing to pronounce them all fictions or productions of the imagination, it may be possible to find an explanation in a theory of hydroscopy. It is held that there are some few persons who are hydroscopes by nature—that is to say, are endowed with peculiar sensations which tell them the moment they are near water, whether it be evident or hidden, a concealed watercourse or a subterranean spring. If the existence of such a faculty, however exceptional, be clearly established, it will afford an explanation of certain successes with the divining-rod.

CHAPTER III.

THE MAGIC MIRROR.

THERE is an old superstition, current, probably, in most parts of the country, that the breaking of a mirror will be followed by bad luck—usually a death in the family. This is, doubtless, the survival of a still older superstition—the belief in certain magic qualities of the mirror, which enabled it in certain circumstances to reflect the distant and to forecast the future. Nor was this superstition so childish as were some other popular delusions of old, for it had a certain philosophic basis. It is the peculiar property of the mirror to represent truth; to reproduce faithfully that which is; to show us ourselves as others see us. This is the idea expressed by Hamlet: 'To hold the mirror up to Nature; to show virtue her own feature, scorn her own image, and the very age and body of the time his form and pressure.'

The mirror has been, from time immemorial, a favourite form of charm for the exorcism of devils, and, indeed, to this day some of the African tribes believe that the best defence they have against their extremely ugly devil is a mirror. If they keep one at hand, the devil must see himself in it before he can touch them, and be so terrified at his own ugliness that he will turn tail and flee.

We may take this symbolically—that a man shrinks from his worst self when it is revealed to him; but the untutored mind is prone to mistake symbol for fact. In this way, while the ancient philosophers may have used the mirror as a symbol of the higher nature of man, so polished and clarified that it showed him his lower nature in all its deformity, the crowd came to regard the crystal as an actual instrument of divination.

Some of the oldest romances in the world have to do with the magical operation of the mirror. In the Gesta Romanorum there is a story of a knight who went to Palestine, and who while there was shown by an Eastern magician in a mirror what was going on at home. In the Arabian Nights the story of Prince Ahmed has a variant, an ivory tube through which could be discovered the far-distant—a sort of anticipation of Sam Weller's 'double million magnifying gas microscope of hextra power.'

In the story of Prince Zeyn Alasnam, the enchanted mirror was able to reflect character, and was called the Touchstone of Virtue. Here again we have Hamlet's idea of holding the mirror up to Nature. The young King, Zeyn Alasnam, had eight beautiful statues of priceless value, and he wanted a ninth to make up his set. The difficulty was to find one beautiful enough; but the Prince of Spirits promised to supply one as soon as Zeyn should bring him a maiden at least fifteen years old, and of perfect beauty; only the maiden must not be vain of her charms, and she must never have told an untruth. Zeyn employed his magic mirror, and for a long time without success, as it always became blurred when he looked into it in the presence of a girl. At last he found one whose image was faithfully and brilliantly reflected—whose modesty and truthfulness were attested by the mirror. He took her with reluctance to the Prince of Spirits, because he had fallen in love with her himself; but his faithfulness to the contract was duly rewarded. On returning home, he found that the ninth statue, placed on its pedestal by the Prince of Spirits according to promise, was no cold marble, but the peerless and virtuous maiden whom he had discovered by means of his mirror.

Paracelsus, in one of his treatises on Magic, gives the following account of the uses to which 'the witches and evil spirits' sometimes put the mirror.

'They take a mirror set in a wooden frame and put it into a tub of water, so that it will swim on the top with its face directed towards the sky. On the top of the mirror, and encircling the glass, they lay a cloth saturated with blood, and thus they expose it to the influence of the moon; and this evil influence is thrown towards the moon, and radiating again from the moon, it may bring evil to those who love to look at the moon. The rays of the moon, passing through the ring upon the mirror, become poisoned, and poison the mirror; the mirror throws back the poisoned ether into the atmosphere, and the moon and the mirror poison each other, in the same manner as two malicious persons, by looking at each other, poison each other's souls with their eyes. If a mirror is strongly poisoned in this manner, the witch takes good care of it; and if she desires to injure someone, she takes a waxen image made in his name, she surrounds it with a cloth spotted with blood, and throws the reflex of the mirror through the opening in the middle upon the head of the figure, or upon some other part of its body, using at the same time her evil imagination and curses; and the man whom the image represents may then have his vitality dried up, and his blood poisoned by that evil influence, and he may become diseased and his body covered with boils.'

This, of course, is not divination, but sorcery.

Paracelsus gives very minute directions for the making of a magic mirror. The material should be the 'electrum magicum,' which is a compound of ten parts of pure gold, ten of silver, five of copper, two of tin, two of lead, one part of powdered iron, and five parts of mercury. When the planets Saturn and Mercury conjoin, the lead has to be melted and the mercury added. Then the metal must cool, while you wait for a conjunction of Jupiter with Saturn and Mercury; when that occurs, you melt the amalgam of lead and mercury, and add the tin, previously melted in a separate crucible, at the exact moment of conjunction. Again you wait for a conjunction of either of the above-named planets with the Sun, when you add the gold; with the Moon, when you add the silver; with Venus, when you add the copper. Finally, when a conjunction of either of the planets occurs with Mars, you must complete your mixture with the powdered iron, and stir up the whole molten mass with a dry rod of witch-hazel.

Thus far your metal; but the mirror is not made yet. It must be of about two inches diameter, and must be founded in moulds of fine sand at the moment when a conjunction of Jupiter and Venus occurs. The mirror must be smoothed with a grindstone and polished with tripoly and a piece of lime-wood; but all the operations must be conducted only when the planetary influences are favourable.

By selecting the proper hours, three different mirrors may be prepared, and then, at a time of conjunction of two 'good' planets, while the Sun or Moon 'stands on the house of the lord of the hour of your birth,' the three mirrors should be placed in pure well-water and left for an hour. After this they may be wrapped in clean linen and kept ready for use.

With a mirror made in this way from the 'electrum magicum,' Paracelsus says:

'You may see the events of the past and the present, absent friends or enemies, and see what they are doing. You may see in it any object you may desire to see, and all the doings of men in daytime or at night. You may see in it anything that has been ever written down, said, or spoken in the past, and also see the person who said it, and the causes that made him say what he did, and you may see in it anything, however secret it may have been kept.'

Mirrors made of the 'electrum magicum' are warranted antipathetic to all evil influences, because there is hidden in the metal a 'heavenly power and influence of the seven planets.'

The plastic and creative power of the mind is the power of imagination; but the power of imagination is, or should be, controlled by the will. It is not alone the mediæval dabblers in the occult who have adopted, or endeavoured to adopt, various means for suspending the will and making the imagination passive.

The ancient Pythoness, as Dr. Franz Hartmann, the modern German exponent of the Science of Magic, pointed out, attempted to heighten her receptivity by the inhalation of noxious vapours; uncivilized peoples use poison, or the maddening whirl of the dance; others use opium, Indian hemp, or other narcotics—all for the same purpose, to suspend the will, render the mind a blank, and excite the brain so as to produce morbid fancies and illusions. The fortune-teller and the clairvoyant employ methods of their own for concentrating their attention, so as produce a condition of mental passivity. The Indian adept prides himself on being able to extract volition and suspend imagination by the mere exercise of will.

A favourite device to bring about mental passivity has always been by staring at mirrors, or crystal, or sheets of water, or even pools of ink.

'There are numerous prescriptions for the preparation of magic mirrors,' says Dr. Hartmann in his work on Magic, 'but the best magic mirror will be useless to him who is not able to see clairvoyantly, while the natural clairvoyant may call that faculty into action by concentrating his mind on any particular spot, a glass of water, ink, a crystal, or anything else. For it is not in the mirror where such things are seen, but in the mind; the mirror merely serves to assist in the entering of that mental state which is necessary to produce clairvoyant sight. The best of all mirrors is the soul of man, and it should be always kept pure, and be protected against dust, and dampness, and rust, so that it may not become tarnished, but remain perfectly clear, and able to reflect the light of the divine spirit in its original purity.'

A German writer of the fifteenth century takes a less favourable view of what he calls pyromancy, although pyromancy is really divination by fire. He reports the practices of certain Masters of Magic, who made children look into a wretched mirror for the purpose of obtaining information in an unholy manner. 'Young boys are said to behold future things and all things, in a crystal. Base, desperate, and faint-hearted Christians practise it, to whom the shadow and the phantom of the devil are dearer than the truth of God. Some take a clear and beautifully polished crystal, or beryl, which they consecrate and keep clean, and treat with incense, myrrh, and the like. And when they propose to practise their art, they wait for a clear day, or select some clean chamber in which are many candles burning. The Masters then bathe, and take the pure child into the room with them, and clothe themselves in pure white garments, and sit down and speak in magic sentences, and then burn their magic offering, and make the boy look into the stone, and whisper in his ears secret words which have, as they think, some holy import, but which are verily words of the devil.'

A sixteenth-century German tells of a man at Elbingen, in Prussia, who 'predicted hidden truths' by means of a mirror, and sold the knowledge to his customers. Many crystal-seeing old hags are referred to as being upon terms of intimacy with Black Kaspar. Indeed, in German literature, both historical, philosophical, legendary, and romantic, we find endless references to the magic mirror and the divining crystal.

Modern romancists still find dramatic use for the old superstitions. Quite recently a novel of the present day centred its interest upon an ancient mirror, which exchanged its reflection for the mind of him who gazed into it—a practical and startling realization of the idea that the glass reveals one's true self. Then, not to multiply incidents, Wilkie Collins, in The Moonstone, introduces what Mr. Rudyard Kipling in another story calls the 'ink-pool'; and readers of Dante Gabriel Rossetti will recall to mind the doings of the Spirits of the Beryl.

In a large number of stories the magic mirror is not a looking-glass at all. But the beryl, the ink-pool, Dr. Dee's famous spherical speculum, the rock crystal, or even a glass of water, may all, according to the adepts, have the same properties as Vulcan's mirror, in which Penelope, the wife of Ulysses, beheld, according to Sir John Davies, a vision of all the wonder and grandeur of Queen Elizabeth's Court to be. Even a polished sword-blade has been asserted to have made an effective magic mirror, and it is recorded that Jacob Boehme penetrated into the innermost secrets of nature and the hearts of men by means of a tin cup.

As to cups, the Septuagint gives one to understand that the cup placed by Joseph in the sack of Benjamin in Egypt was not an ordinary drinking-vessel, but a divining-cup. Now, the way of divining with a cup was to fill it with pure water, and to read the images which were then reflected.

Some writers have supposed, from the mention of Urim and Thummim in Exodus, that divination by mirror was a recognised institution among the Jews. Urim signifies 'lights,' and Thummim 'reflections,' and the names were applied to the six bright and six dark precious stones on the breastplate of the high priest when he went to seek special revelations.

Cambuscan's mirror was, according to Chaucer, of Oriental origin. It was given by the King of Tartary to the King of Araby, and it seemed to possess all the virtues of several kinds of magic mirrors. Thus it showed whether love was returned, whether an individual confronted with it were friend or foe, and what trouble was in store for those who consulted it. Merlin's mirror, also called Venus's looking-glass, had some of these properties, but was made in Wales, and was given by Merlin to King Ryence. It revealed what was being done by friend or foe at a distance, and it also enabled the fair Britomart to read the features, and also the name, of her future husband.

The consultation of a pool, on certain special occasions, for the lineaments of 'the coming man,' has been a common enough practice with love-sick damsels in much more recent times.

The wonderful looking-glass of Lao, described by Lien Chi Altangi in Goldsmith's Citizen of the World, reflected the mind as well as the body, and the Emperor Chusi used to make his ladies dress both their heads and their hearts before it every morning. Great, however, as are the Chinese in divination, and numerous as are their superstitions, we do not find, *pace* Oliver Goldsmith, that the mirror occupies any prominent place in their magic.

One of the most famous dealers in catoptromancy (divination by mirror) in this country was Dr. John Dee, who flourished about the middle of the sixteenth century. He had a speculum called the Shew Stone, and sometimes the Holy Stone, with which he divined by the aid of a medium named Kelly. This Kelly was a notoriously bad character, so his example does not carry out the popular idea that the seer must be a stainless child, or some absolutely pure-minded being. Dr. Dee professed to have a number of regular spirit-visitors, whom he described with much circumstantial minuteness, and thus his mirror-magic seems to have possessed more of the character of spiritualistic manifestations than of the usual Oriental crystallomancy.

The famous Cagliostro—Prince of Scoundrels, as Carlyle called him—used a bottle of pure water, into which he directed a child to gaze, with results which were not always satisfactory.

The Orientalist, Lane, published some sixty years ago, or more, a circumstantial narrative of an experience he had with an Egyptian magician, along with Mr. Salt, a British Consul. Invocations were liberally used, in order to summon the two genii of the magician, and verses were recited from the Koran, in order that the eyes of the medium—a boy—should be opened in a supernatural manner. The magician selected one at random from a group of boys, and drew in the palm of the boy's right hand a magic square, inscribed with Arabic figures. He then poured ink into the centre, and told the boy to gaze fixedly, while he himself proceeded to drop more written invocations, on slips of paper, into a chafing-dish.

For some time the boy saw nothing but the reflection of the magician, and then he began to describe various scenes. At last Lane asked that Lord Nelson should be called up, and the boy said that he saw a man in dark-blue clothes, with his left arm across his breast. It was explained that the boy saw things as in a mirror, and that Nelson's empty right sleeve worn across the breast naturally appeared in the glass as the left arm. Now, the boy may have heard of Nelson, but could scarcely have seen him, though the figure of so famous a man must have been familiar to the magician. Hypnotism has, therefore, been suggested as the explanation of what Lane witnessed, and which seemed so miraculous at the time.

Many scholars, philosophers, and scientific students of mediæval times, who had no pretence to magic, had yet firm faith in the power of mirrors, constructed in a special manner and under auspicious planetary influences, to reveal both the distant-present and the future.

One of the modern adepts was a French magician, who foretold by his mirror the death of a Prince, and the regency of the Duc d'Orleans.

There are many published prescriptions for the making of a magic mirror, but that which has already been given from Paracelsus is a fair specimen of the ultra-scientific method. Among directions for the use of the crystal may be cited those of Barth:

'When a crystal has been ground and polished, it is dedicated to some spirit or other; this is called its consecration. Before being used, it is charged—that is, an invocation is made to the spirit, wherein a vision is requested of the things that one wishes to experience. Ordinarily, a young person is chosen to look into the glass and behold the prayed-for vision. After a little time the crystal becomes enveloped in a cloud, and a tiny vision appears, which represents in miniature the persons, scenes, and things that are necessary to supply the required information. When the information has been obtained, the crystal is discharged, and after receiving thanks for the services he has performed, the spirit is dismissed.'

In modern crystal-gazing and mirror-reading, however, there is no invocation.

An American spiritualist says that he once put a crystal into the hands of a lady who knew nothing about its reputed virtues, but who straightway began to describe a scene which she saw in it, and which turned out afterwards to be a simultaneous incident at Trebizond. The mediumistic influence of the spirit of a North American Indian may not commend the story to non-spiritualists.

The experiences of the Countess Wurmbrand, as related in her curious book, Visionen im Wasserglass, are more matter-of-fact, perhaps, but were also assisted by a mysterious spirit, who enabled her to read pictures in the glass and to describe them to her husband. She was more successful in her time than more recent experimenters and psychologists of her own country have been since.

The Society for Psychical Research have given much attention to the subject, and have reported some remarkable observations—especially those of Miss Goodrich, a lady who has made several scores of experiments of her own in crystal-reading, always taking notes immediately. She tried the back of a watch, a glass of water, a mirror, and other reflecting surfaces, before arriving at the conclusion that polished rock crystal affords the best speculum for divination.

Having reached this point, the lady draped her selected crystal in black, set it where no surrounding objects could be reflected in it, and sought it when in search of light and leading. Sometimes her consultations were very practical. Thus, one finds among her notes:

'I had carelessly destroyed a letter without preserving the address of my correspondent. I knew the county, and searching a map, recognised the name of the town, one unfamiliar to me, but which I was sure I should know when I saw it. But I had no clue to the name of the house or street, till at last it struck me to test the value of the crystal as a means of recalling forgotten knowledge. A very short inspection supplied me with "Hibbs House," in gray letters on a white ground, and having nothing better to suggest from any other source, I risked posting my letter to the address so strangely supplied. A day or two brought an answer headed "Hibbs House" in gray letters on a white ground.'

Let us take an example of another of Miss Goodrich's crystal-readings, and let it be remembered that they are all reported as experiments of our own day:

'One of my earliest experiences was of a picture, perplexing and wholly unexpected—a quaint oak chair, an old hand, a worn black coat-sleeve resting on the arm of the chair—slowly recognised as a recollection of a room in a country vicarage which I had not entered, and but seldom recalled, since I was a child of ten. But whence came this vision? What association has conjured up this picture? What have I done to-day? At length the clue is found. I have to-day been reading Dante, first enjoyed with the help of our dear old vicar many a year ago.'

And again: 'I happened to want the date of Ptolemy Philadelphus, which I could not recall, though feeling sure that I knew it, and that I associated it with some event of importance. When looking in the crystal, some hours later, I found a picture of an old man, with long, white hair and beard, dressed like a Lyceum Shylock, and busy writing in a large book with tarnished massive clasps. I wondered much who he was, and what he could possibly be doing, and thought it a good opportunity of carrying out a suggestion which had been made to me of examining objects in the crystal with a magnifying-glass. The glass revealed to me that my old gentleman was writing in Greek, though the lines faded away as I looked, all but the characters he had last traced, the Latin numerals LXX. Then it flashed into my mind that he was one of the Jewish Elders at work on the Septuagint, and that this date, 277 B.C., would serve equally well for Ptolemy Philadelphus. It may be worth while to add, though the fact was not in my conscious memory at the moment, that I had once learnt a chronology on a mnemonic system which substituted letters for figures, and the *memoria technica* for this date was, "Now Jewish Elders indite a Greek copy."'

One may, perhaps, find a simple and easy explanation of Miss Goodrich's mirror-reading, in a theory of unconscious cerebration. The crystal simply assisted her memory, and recalled incidents and scenes, just as a chance odour, a bar of music, a word, a look, a name, will often do for most of us. Clearly there is nothing necessarily either magic or spiritualistic in this particular example of the magic mirror.

There are, however, some other experiments recorded which seem to be only explainable on a theory of telepathy; but Mr. Max Dessoir, commenting on the evidence of Miss Goodrich in an American Review, attributes the whole phenomena merely to 'revived memory.'

This is all very well as to past events, but what shall we say to a case such as the following, among Miss Goodrich's experiments?

'In January last I saw in the crystal the figure of a man crouching at a small window, and looking into the room from the outside. I could not see his features, which appeared to be muffled, but the crystal was particularly dark that evening, and the picture being an unpleasant one, I did not persevere. I concluded the vision to be a result of a discussion in my presence of the many stories of burglary with which the newspapers had lately abounded, and reflected with a passing satisfaction that the only windows in the house divided into four panes, as were those of the crystal picture, were in the front attic, and almost inaccessible. Three days later a fire broke out in that very room, which had to be entered from outside through the window, the face of the fireman being covered with a wet cloth as a protection from the smoke, which rendered access through the door impossible.'

Was this coincidence, or prevision, or what Mr. Dessoir calls the 'falsification of memory'? The thing was either a miracle, which none of us is prepared to accept, or the after-confusion of a vague foreboding with an actual occurrence in the mind of the observer. Mr. Dessoir suggested another explanation of crystal pictures in the doctrine of the double consciousness of the human soul; but that opens up another subject.

While we have seen that mirror and crystal-reading is one of the most ancient of occult practices, we have also seen that it is practised in our own country even at this day. Moreover, it is said that there is in England a wholesale manufacture of magic mirrors as a regular industry—the site of which, however, the present writer is unable to specify.

CHAPTER IV.

THE MAGIC MOON.

CERTAINLY since, and probably long before, Job 'beheld the moon walking in brightness,' all the peoples of the earth have surrounded that luminary with legends, with traditions, with myths, and with superstitions of various kinds. In our time, and in our own country, the sentiment with which the orb of night is regarded is a soft and pleasing one, for

'That orbèd maiden, with white fire laden,
Whom mortals call the moon,'

is supposed to look with approval upon happy lovers, and with sympathy upon those who are encountering the proverbial rough places in the course of true love. Why the moon should be partial to lovers one might easily explain on very prosaic grounds—perhaps not unlike the reasoning of the Irishman who called the sun a coward because he goes away as soon as it begins to grow dark, whereas the blessed moon stays with us most of the night!

Except Lucian and M. Jules Verne, one does not readily recall anyone who professes to have been actually up to the moon. Lucian had by far the most eventful experience, for he met Endymion, who entertained him royally, and did all the honours of the planet to which he had been wafted from earth in his sleep. The people of Moonland, Lucian assures us, live upon flying frogs, only they do not eat them; they cook the frogs on a fire and swallow the smoke. For drink, he says, they pound air in a mortar, and thus obtain a liquid very like dew. They have vines, only the grapes yield not wine, but water, being, in fact, hailstones, such as descend upon the earth when the wind shakes the vines in the moon. Then the Moonfolk have a singular habit of taking out their eyes when they do not wish to see things—a habit which has its disadvantages, for sometimes they mislay their eyes and have to borrow a pair from their neighbours. The rich, however, provide against such accidents by always keeping a good stock of eyes on hand.

Lucian also discovered the reason of the red clouds which we on earth often see at sunset. They are dyed by the immense quantity of blood which is shed in the battles between the Moonfolk and the Sunfolk, who are at constant feud.

The reason why the gentler sex are so fond of the moon is satirically said to be because there is a man in it! But who and what is he? An old writer, John Lilly, says: 'There liveth none under the sunne that knows what to make of the man in the moone.' And yet many have tried.

One old ballad, for instance, says:

'The man in the moon drinks claret,
But he is a dull Jack-a-Dandy.
Would he know a sheep's head from a carrot,
He should learn to drink cyder and brandy'

—which may be interesting, but is certainly inconsequential. It is curious, too, that while the moon is feminine in English, French, Latin and Greek, it is masculine in German and cognate tongues. Now, if there is a man in the moon, and if it be the case, as is asserted by antiquarians, that the 'man in the moon' is one of the most ancient as well as one of the most popular superstitions of the world, the masculine is surely the right gender after all. Those who look to Sanscrit for the solution of all mythological, as well as philological, problems will confirm this, for in Sanscrit the moon is masculine. Dr. Jamieson, of Scottish Dictionary fame, gets out of the difficulty by saying that the moon was regarded as masculine in relation to the earth, whose husband he was; but feminine in relation to the sun, whose wife she was!

With the Greeks the moon was a female, Diana, who caught up her lover Endymion; and Endymion was thus, probably, the first 'man in the moon.' The Jews, again, have a tradition that Jacob is in the moon; and there is the nursery story that the person in the moon is a man who was condemned for gathering sticks on Sunday. This myth comes to us from Germany—at all events, Mr. R. A. Proctor traced it there with much circumstantiality. Mr. Baring-Gould, however, finds in some parts of Germany a tradition that both a man and a woman are in the moon—the man because he strewed brambles and thorns on the church path to hinder people from attending Sunday mass, and the woman because she made butter on Sunday. This man carries two bundles of thorns, and the woman her butter-tub, for ever. In Swabia they say there is a mannikin in the moon, who stole wood; and in Frisia they say it is a man, who stole cabbages. The Scandinavian legend is that the moon and sun are brother and sister—the moon in this case being the male. The story goes that Mâni, the moon, took up two children from earth, named Bil and Hjuki, as they were carrying a pitcher of water from the well Brygir, and in this myth Mr. Baring-Gould discovers the origin of the nursery rhyme of Jack and Jill. 'These children,' he says, 'are the moon-spots, and the fall of Jack, and the subsequent fall of Jill, simply represent the vanishing of one moon-spot after another as the moon wanes.'

In Britain there are references in the ancient monkish writings to a man in the moon; and in the Record Office there is an impression of a seal of the fourteenth century bearing the device of a man carrying a bundle of thorns in the moon. The legend attached is, 'Te Waltere docebo cur spinas phebo gero' ('I will teach thee, Walter, why I carry thorns to the moon'), which Mr. Hudson Taylor, who describes the seal, thinks to be an enigmatical way of saying that honesty is the best policy—the thorns having evidently been stolen.

Chaucer has more than one reference to the man in the moon, and so have most of the older poets. Shakespeare not only refers frequently to 'a' man, but in the Midsummer Night's Dream Peter Quince distinctly stipulates that the man who is to play 'the moon' shall carry 'a bush of thorns.'

The man in the moon, according to Dante, is Cain, carrying a bundle of thorns, and yet in that planet he found located only those comparatively mild sinners who had partly neglected their vows. A French legend, on the other hand, identifies 'the man' with Judas Iscariot. *Per contra*, in India the Buddhist legend places a hare in the moon, carried there by Indra for kindly service rendered to him on earth.

May not this hare of the Indian mythology be the moon-dog of some of our own legends? Peter Quince, we know, recommended that the moon should have a dog as well as a bundle of sticks, and the association of the quadruped in the story is very common. The North American Indians believe that the moon is inhabited by a man and a dog. The Maoris believe in the man, but not in the dog, which is not surprising when we remember the limited fauna of the antipodes. The Maori legend runs something like this. A man called Rona went out one night to fetch water from a well, but, falling, sprained his ankle so as to be unable to return home. All at once the moon, which had risen, began to approach him. In terror he clung to a tree, which gave way, and both tree and Rona fell on the moon, where they remain even unto this day. Here we have clearly a variation of the 'bundle of sticks' legend, but there is an absence of apparent cause and effect in the Maori legend which is unsatisfactory.

More precise is the Bushman legend, quoted by Dr. Bleek. According to this, the moon is a man who incurs the wrath of the sun, and is consequently pierced by the knife (the rays) of the latter, until there is only a little piece of him left. Then he cries for mercy for his children's sake, and is allowed to grow again until once more he offends his sunship; the whole process being repeated monthly.

Dr. Rink relates a curious tradition of the Eskimo, not quite quotable here, the gist of which is that a man who desired to make his sister his wife was transformed into the moon, while the woman became the sun. Something like the same legend has been traced as far south as Panama. Another notable thing about Eskimo traditions is that the moon is associated with fertility in woman. This superstition is both very ancient and very widespread, and, indeed, seems to have been the root both of the moon-worship of the Oriental nations and of the mysterious rites of the Egyptians referred to by Herodotus. Luna is identified by some mythologists with Soma of the Indian mythology, *i.e.*, the emblem of reproduction.

In China, according to Dr. Dennys, the man in the moon is called Yue-lao, and he is believed to hold in his hands the power of predestining marriages. He is supposed to tie together the future husband and wife with an invisible silken cord, which never parts while life lasts. Miss Gordon-Cumming, in her interesting account of Wanderings in China, relates that, in the neighbourhood of Foo-Chow, she witnessed a great festival being held in honour of the full moon, which was mainly attended by women. There was a Temple-play, or sing-song, going on all day and most of the night, and each woman carried a stool so that she might sit out the whole performance. This recalls what Mr. Riley states in The Book of Days, as related by John Andrey in the seventeenth century: 'In Scotland, especially among the Highlanders, the women make a courtesy to the new moon, and our English women in this country have a touch of this, some of them sitting astride on a gate or stile the first evening the new moon appears, and saying, "A fine moon! God bless her!" The like I observed in Herefordshire.'

As illustrative of this superstition may be instanced a curious practice in this country, in olden times, of divination by the moon. It is quoted by Mr. Thiselton-Dyer from an old chap-book: 'When you go to bed (at the period of harvest moon) place under your pillow a Prayer-Book open at the part of the matrimonial service, which says, "With this ring I thee wed"; place on it a key, a ring, a flower, and a sprig of willow, a small heart-cake, a crust, and the following cards: a ten of clubs, nine of hearts, ace of spades, and ace of diamonds. Wrap all these in a thin handkerchief, and, on getting into bed, cover your hands, and say:

"Luna, every woman's friend,
To me thy goodness condescend:
Let me this night in visions see
Emblems of my destiny."

It is certainly hard to imagine pleasant dreams as the result of such a very uncomfortably-stuffed pillow.

In this same connection may be named other items of folklore related by Mr. Dyer. For instance, in Devonshire it is believed that if on seeing the first new moon of the year you take off one stocking and run across a field, you will find between two of your toes a hair which will be the colour of the lover you are to have. In Berkshire the proceeding is more simple, for you merely look at the new moon, and say:

'New moon, new moon, I hail thee!
By all the virtue in thy body,
Grant this night that I may see
He who my true love shall be!'

The result is guaranteed to be as satisfactory as it is in Ireland, where the people are said to point to the new moon with a knife, and say:

'New moon, true morrow, be true now to me,
That I to-morrow my true love may see!'

In Yorkshire, again, the practice was to catch the reflection of the new moon in a looking-glass, the number of reflections signifying the number of years which will elapse before marriage. All these superstitions are suggestive of that which Tylor calls 'one of the most instructive astrological doctrines'—namely, that of the 'sympathy of growing and declining nature with the waxing and waning moon.' Tylor says that a classical precept was to set eggs under the hen at new moon, and that a Lithuanian precept was to wean boys on a waxing and girls on a waning moon—in order to make the boys strong and the girls delicate. On the same grounds, he says, Orkney-men object to marry except with a growing moon, and Mr. Dyer says that in Cornwall, when a child is born in the interval between an old and a new moon, it is believed that he will never live to manhood.

Dr. Turner relates several traditions of the moon current in Samoa. There is one of a visit paid to the planet by two young men—Punifanga, who went up by a tree, and Tafaliu, who went up on a column of smoke. There is another of a woman, Sina, who was busy one evening cutting mulberry-bark for cloth with her child beside her. It was a time of famine, and the rising moon reminded her of a great bread-fruit—just as in our country it has reminded some people of a green cheese. Looking up, she said: 'Why cannot you come down and let my child have a bit of you?' The moon was so indignant at being taken for an article of food, that she came down forthwith and took up woman, child and wood. There they are to this day, for in the full moon the Samoans still see the features of Sina, the face of the child, and the board and mallet.

Mr. Andrew Lang finds in an Australian legend of the moon something oddly like Grimm's tale of the Wolf and the Kids, which, again, he likens to the old Greek myth of Cronos. The Australian legend is that birds were the original gods, and that the eagle especially was a great creative power. The moon was a mischievous being, who walked about the earth doing all the evil he could. One day he swallowed the eagle. The eagle's wives coming up, the moon asked where he could find a well. They pointed out one, and while he was drinking, they struck him with a stone tomahawk, which made him disgorge the eagle. This legend is otherwise suggestive from the circumstances that among the Greeks the eagle was the special bird of Zeus, and it was the eagle which carried off Ganymede.

There is another Australian fable that the moon was a man, and the sun a woman of doubtful reputation who appears at dawn in a coat of red kangaroo-skin belonging to one of her lovers. In Mexico, also, the moon is a man, across whose face an angry immortal once threw a rabbit; hence the marks on the surface of the planet. These same marks are accounted for in the Eskimo legend already mentioned as the impressions of the woman's sooty fingers on the face of her pursuer. By some mythologists the moon is thought to be Medea, but it is more common to interpret Medea as the daughter of the sun, *i.e.*, the dawn.

It is certainly not a little curious to find the moon-lore, as the star-lore, having so many points of resemblance among such widely-separated and different peoples as the Greeks, the Egyptians, the Australians, the Eskimos, the Bushmen of South Africa, the North American Indians, and the New Zealand Maoris. The comparative mythologists would argue from this resemblance a common origin of the myth, and a distribution or communication from one race to the other. The folk-lore mythologists would infer nothing of the sort. They say there is nothing remarkable in all savage races imputing human motives and sex to the heavenly bodies, for, in fact, to this day there are savages, as in the South Pacific, who suppose even stones to be male and female, and to propagate their species. On this method of interpretation the hypothesis is not that the Australians, Indians, etc., received their myths from, say, the Greeks, either by community of stock or by contact and borrowing, but because the ancestors of the Greeks passed through the same intellectual condition as the primitive races we now know. And thus it is that in listening to the beautiful legends of the Greeks, we are but, as Bacon says, hearing the harsh ideas of earlier peoples 'blown softly through the flutes of the Grecians.'

Now, beside the personality of the moon, and the peculiar influence he or she is supposed to exercise on mortals, there has survived an old superstition that the moon has direct influence on the weather. Apropos of this association, there is a pretty little Hindoo legend which is current in Southern India, and which has been translated by Miss Frere, daughter of Sir Bartle Frere. This is the story as told her by her Lingaet ayah:

'One day the Sun, the Moon, and the Wind went out to dine with their uncle and aunt, the Thunder and Lightning. Their mother (one of the most distant stars you see far up in the sky) waited alone for her children's return. Now, both the Sun and the Wind were greedy and selfish. They enjoyed the great feast that had been prepared for them, without a thought of saving any of it to take home to their mother; but the gentle Moon did not forget her. Of every dainty dish that was brought round she placed a small portion under one of her beautiful long fingernails, that the Star might also have a share in the treat. On their return, their mother, who had kept watch for them all night long with her bright little eye, said: "Well, children, what have you brought home for me?" Then the Sun (who was eldest) said: "I have brought nothing home for you. I went out to enjoy myself with my friends, not to fetch a dinner for my mother!" And the Wind said: "Neither have I brought anything home for you, mother. You could hardly expect me to bring a collection of good things for you, when I merely went out for my own pleasure." But the Moon said: "Mother, fetch a plate; see what I have brought you;" and shaking her hands, she showered down such a choice dinner as never was seen before. Then the Star turned to the Sun, and spoke thus: "Because you went out to amuse yourself with your friends, and feasted and enjoyed yourself without any thought of your mother at home, you shall be cursed. Henceforth your rays shall ever be hot and scorching, and shall burn all that they touch. All men shall hate you, and cover their heads when you appear"; and this is why the sun is so hot to this day. Then she turned to the Wind, and said: "You also, who forgot your mother in the midst of your selfish pleasures, hear your doom. You shall always blow in the hot, dry weather, and shall parch and shrivel all living things, and men shall detest and avoid you from this very time"; and this is why the wind in the hot weather is still so disagreeable. But to the Moon she said: "Daughter, because you remembered your mother, and kept for her a share in your own enjoyment, from henceforth you shall be ever cool, and calm, and bright. No noxious glare shall accompany your pure rays, and men shall always call you blessed"; and that is why the moon's light is so soft, and cool, and beautiful even to this day.'

It is remarkable, nevertheless, that among Western peoples, at any rate, the moon has usually been associated with the uncanny. It is an old belief, for instance, that the moon is the abode of bad spirits; and in the old story of the Vampire it is notable that the creature, as a last request, begged that he might be buried where no sunlight, but only moonlight, might fall on his grave. Witches were supposed to be able to control the moon, as witness the remark of Prospero in The Tempest:

'His mother was a witch, and one so strong,
That could control the moon.'

The Rev. Timothy Harley, who has collected much moon-lore, suggests that if the broom on which witches rode to the moon be a type of the wind, 'we may guess how the fancy grew up that the airy creation could control those atmospheric vapours on which the light and humidity of the night were supposed to depend.'

But the 'glamour' of the moon is not a mere poetic invention or a lover's fancy. Mr. Moncure Conway reminds us that *glám*, in its nominative form *glámir*, is a poetical name for the moon, to be found in the Prose Edda. It is given in the Glossary as one of the old names for the moon. Mr. Conway also says that there is a curious old Sanscrit word, *glau* or *gláv*, which is explained in all the old lexicons as meaning the moon. Hence 'the ghost or goblin Glam (of the old legend of Grettir) seems evidently to have arisen from a personification of the delusive and treacherous effects of moonlight on the benighted traveller.'

Similar delusive effects are found referred to in old Hindoo writings, as, for instance, in the following passages from Bhása, a poet of the seventh century:

'The cat laps the moonbeams in the bowl of water, thinking them to be milk; the elephant thinks that the moonbeams threaded through the intervals of the trees are the fibres of the lotus-stalk; the woman snatches at the moonbeams as they lie on the bed, taking them for her muslin garment. Oh, how the moon, intoxicated with radiance, bewilders all the world!'

Again:

'The bewildered herdsmen place the pails under the cows, thinking that the milk is flowing; the maidens also put the blue lotus-blossom in their ears, thinking that it is the white; the mountaineer's wife snatches up the jujube fruit, avaricious for pearls. Whose mind is not led astray by the thickly-clustering moonbeams?'

Such was the 'glamour' of Glam (the moon) in ancient eyes, and still it works on lovers' hearts. The fascination has been felt and expressed by nearly all the poets, and by none better, perhaps, than by Sir Philip Sidney:

'With what sad steps, O moon, thou climb'st the skies!
How silently, and with how wan a face!
What, may it be, that even in heavenly place
That busy archer his sharp arrow tries?
Sure if that long with love-acquainted eyes
Can judge of love, thou feel'st a lover's case.

I read it in thy looks—thy languish'd grace
To me, that feel the like, thy state descries.'

The number of human beings who have, articulately or inarticulately, cried with Endymion, 'What is there in thee, Moon, that thou should'st move my heart so potently?' are not to be measured in ordinary figures.

To return, however, to the bad side of Luna's character. We read that in Assyria deadly influences were ascribed to the moon. In Vedic mythology there is a story, which Mr. Moncure Conway tells in Demonology and Devil-lore, of a quarrel between Brahma and Vishnu as to which was the first born. Siva interferes, and says he is the first born, but will recognise as his superior whoever is able to see the crown of his head or the soles of his feet. Vishnu thereupon transforms himself into a boar, pierces underground, and thus sees the feet of Siva, who salutes him on his return as the firstborn of the gods. Now, De Gubernatis regards this fable as 'making the boar emblem of the hidden moon'; and Mr. Conway thinks there is no doubt that the boar at an early period became emblematic of the wild forces of Nature. 'From being hunted by King Odin on earth, it passed to be his favourite food in Valhalla, and a prominent figure in his spectral hunt.' But it is with the moon, not with Odin, that we are at present concerned, and so note two curious items mentioned by Conway. In Sicilian legend, he says, 'Zafarana, by throwing three hog's bristles on embers, renews her husband's youth'; and in Esthonian legend, a prince, by eating pork, acquires the faculty of understanding the language of birds. All this opens up a very suggestive field of inquiry. Thus, Plutarch says that the reason why the Jews would not eat swine's flesh was because Adonis was slain by a boar, and Bacchus and Adonis, he says, were the same divinities. Now, if we turn to Herodotus, we find that wonderful narrator saying: 'The only deities to whom the Egyptians offer swine are Bacchus and Luna; to these they sacrifice swine when the moon is full, after which they eat the flesh,' which at other times they disdained. The meaning of these sacrifices is understood by those interested, and I do not propose to go further into the matter. All I wish to do is to point out the curious involvements, among so many nations, of the moon and the boar.

May we not even trace a connection with the superstition current in Suffolk, according to 'C. W. J.,' in The Book of Days? 'C. W. J.' says that in his part of the world it is considered unlucky to kill a pig when the moon is on the wane; and if it is done, the pork will waste in boiling. 'I have known,' he says, 'the shrinking of bacon in the pot attributed to the fact of the pig having been killed in the moon's decrease; and I have also known the death of poor piggy delayed or hastened so as to happen during its increase.' Truly the old superstitions die hard!

The moon's supposed influence on the weather is a matter of general knowledge. The writer last quoted mentions it as a very prevalent belief that the general condition of the atmosphere throughout the world, during any lunation, depends on whether the moon changed before or after midnight. Another superstition is, that if the new moon happens on a Saturday the weather will be bad during the month. On the other hand, in Suffolk the old moon in the arms of the new one is accounted a sign of fine weather; contrary to the belief in Scotland, where, it may be remembered, in the ballad of Sir Patrick Spens, it is taken as a presage of storm and disaster.

Shakespeare has many allusions to the moon's influence on the weather, as: 'The moon, the governess of floods, pale in her anger, washes the air'; 'The moon, one thinks, looks with a watery eye; and when she weeps, weeps every little flower'; 'Upon the corner of the moon there hangs a vaporous drop profound'; and so forth. Then we have the old proverb: 'So many days old the moon is on Michaelmas Day, so many floods after.' Other beliefs are mentioned by Mr. Harley, such as, that if Christmas comes during a waning moon, we shall have a good year, and the converse; that new moon on Monday is a certain sign of good weather; that a misty moon indicates heavy rain; that the horns of the moon turned upward predict a good, and turned downward a bad, season; that a large star near the moon is a certain prognostication of storm.

In fact, the superstitions in this connection are legion, and are not confined to any country. They are as common in China, where the moon is still worshipped, as they are in England, where, in some places, old men still touch their hats and maidens still bob a courtesy in sight of the new moon. Thus the relics of moon-worship are about us still, as well as a strong popular belief that the moon is an active physical agent. That the actual influence of the moon on the tides lies at the basis of the belief in its influence on the weather is probable; and, at any rate, it is curious that the Persians held that the moon was the cause of an abundant supply of water and rain; while in a Japanese fairy-tale the moon is made to rule over the blue waste of the sea with its multitudinous salt waters. The horticultural superstitions about sowing and planting according to the age of the moon is, no doubt, a product of the fusion of the meteorological superstition and that of the old-world belief in Luna being the goddess of reproduction.

Any who have still doubts on the meteorological question cannot do better than refer to a letter of Professor Nichol's—once Professor of Astronomy in the University of Glasgow—which is quoted in The Book of Days. He asserts positively, as the result of scientific observation, that no relation whatever exists between the moon and the weather.

But does any exist between the moon and the brain? 'Whom the gods would destroy, they first make mad'; and the moon was supposed to be the instrument—nay, still is, as the very word 'lunacy' implies. The old astrologers used to say that she governed the brain, stomach, bowels, and left eye of the male, and the right eye of the female. Some such influences were evidently believed in by the Jews, as witness Psalm cxxi.: 'The sun shall not smite thee by day, nor the moon by night.' It may be remarked that Dr. Forbes Winslow is not very decided in dismissing the theory of the influence of the moon on the insane. He says it is purely speculative, but he does not controvert it. The subject is, however, too large to enter upon here. Whether or not it be true that 'when the moon's in the full then wit's on the wane,' it certainly is not true, as appears to be believed in Sussex, that the new May Moon has power to cure scrofulous complaints.

Before leaving the subject, it is well to mention a remarkable coincidence to which Mr. Harley draws attention. In China, where moon-worship largely prevails, during the festival of Yue-Ping, which is held during the eighth month annually, incense is burned in the temples, cakes are made like the moon, and at full moon the people spread out oblations and make prostrations to the planet. These cakes are moon-cakes, and veritable offerings to the Queen of Heaven, who represents the female principle in Chinese theology. 'If we turn now to Jeremiah vii. 18, and read there, "The women knead dough to make cakes to the Queen of Heaven, and to pour out drink-offerings unto other gods," and remember that, according to Rashi, these cakes of the Hebrews had the image of the god or goddess stamped upon them, we are in view of a fact of much interest.' The interest becomes greater when we learn that in parts of Lancashire there exists a precisely similar custom of making cakes in honour of the Queen of Heaven.

From these facts, the discovery of two buns, each marked with a cross, in Herculaneum, and other evidences, we are driven to the conclusion that the 'hot-cross buns' of Christian England are in reality but a relic of moon-worship!

CHAPTER V.

THE DEVIL'S CANDLE.

SO much legendary lore and so many strange fables have had their origin in the mandrake, or the 'Devil's Candle,' as the Arabians call it, that it is worth while to endeavour to trace if any, and what, analogy there be between it and the mandragoras of the Greeks and the Soma of the Indian mythology.

The mandrake is so called from the German *Mandragen*, 'resembling man'— at least, so says Mr. Thiselton-Dyer; but this derivation is not quite satisfactory. The botanical name is *Mandragora officinalis*, and sometimes the May-apple, or *Podophyllum peltatum*, is also called mandrake; but the actual plant of fact and fancy belongs to the *Solanum*, or potato family.

Although one may doubt if the English name be really derived from the German *Mandragen*, it is certain that the Germans have long regarded the plant as something uncanny. Other names which they have for it are *Zauberwurzel*, or Sorcerer's Root, and *Hexenmännchen*, or Witch's Mannikin, while they made little dolls or idols from it, which they regarded with superstitious veneration, and called *Erdmann*, or Earth-man.

Yet in other places, according to one authority, the mandrake was popularly supposed to be 'perpetually watched over by Satan; and if it be pulled up at certain holy times and with certain invocations, the evil spirit will appear to do the bidding of the practitioner.' A superstition once common in the South of England was that the mandrake had a human heart at its root, and, according to Timbs, it was generally believed that the person who pulled it would instantaneously fall dead; that the root shrieked or groaned whenever separated from the earth; and that whoever heard the shriek would either die shortly afterwards or become afflicted with madness.

To this last superstition there is direct reference made by Shakespeare in Romeo and Juliet:

'And shrieks like mandrakes torn out of the earth,
That living mortals hearing them run mad.'

Frequent allusions to this superstition are to be found in the old poets, although it is held by some that the effects claimed for decoctions of the mandrake really refer to those of the nightshade. This confusion has certainly arisen at times, but the most general idea concerning the mandrake was that it was a stimulant rather than a narcotic. It is true that Shakespeare regarded mandragora as an opiate, for he makes Cleopatra to exclaim:

'Give me to drink mandragora,
That I might sleep out this great gap of time
My Antony is away.'

And, again, when in Othello he makes Iago say:

'Nor poppy, nor mandragora,
Nor all the drowsy syrups of the world
Can ever medicine thee to that sweet sleep
Which thou owedst yesterday.'

But, on the other hand, we find Apuleius—himself, by the way, not unsuspected of magical arts—writing that when the root of the mandrake is steeped in wine it produces vehement intoxication. The same idea is reflected in Mrs. Browning's Dead Pan:

'In what revels are ye sunken
In old Ethiopia?
Have the Pygmies made you drunken,
Bathing in mandragora,
Your divine pale lips that shiver
Like the lotus in the river?'

And there can be little doubt that the mysterious 'Lhasis,' referred to by Sir William Davenant[5]—a word whose etymology is so obscure—is nothing else than the mandrake or mandragora; if so, then we see that the plant was valued for its exciting and stimulating effects rather than as an opiate.

Many commentators and most dictionaries dispose of Reuben's mandrakes as something altogether different from the plant now known by the name; but there is really no warrant for such a conclusion. The *Mandragora officinalis* is quite common in Celicia, Syria, and elsewhere in the East, and is easily identifiable with the root of Baaras, which Josephus describes in the Wars of the Jews. This root, he says, is in colour like to that of flame, and towards the evening it sends out a certain ray like lightning. It is not easily to be pulled, it will not yield quietly, and it is certain death to anyone who dares pull it, unless he hangs it with the head downwards. As to the uses of the root, Josephus continues: 'After all his pains in getting it, it is only valuable on account of one virtue it hath: that if it only be brought to sick persons, it quickly drives away those called Demons, which are no other than the spirits of the wicked, which enter into men that are alive and kill them, unless they can obtain some help against them'; and the root was esteemed a useful stimulant, although in Baaras, at any rate, it seems to have lost its reputation as a love-philtre. It is noteworthy that Josephus also tells how Solomon had great skill in enchantments, and cast out devils by means of this root—an accomplishment he is said to have learned from some of the numerous foreign ladies with whom he surrounded himself.

Now, it is interesting to turn from the old Jewish historian to the old English herbalist, Gerarde, who in 1597 wrote in his Herball pointing out how, by 'the corruption of time and the errour of some,' mandragora has been mistaken for what he calls Circaea, or Enchanter's Nightshade. But of the mandrake, or mandragoras, Gerarde says: 'There hath been many ridiculous tales brought up of this plant, whether of old wives, or some runagate surgeons, or physickemongers, I know not; but sure some one or more that sought to make themselves famous or skillful above others were the first brochers of the errour'—that the root resembles a man. 'They add further,' he says, 'that it is never, or very seldome, to be found growing naturally, but under a gallowes, where the matter that hath fallen from the dead body hath given it the shape of a man, and the matter of a woman the substance of a female plant, with many other such doltish dreames. The fable further affirms that he who would take up a plant thereof ... he should surely die in short space after.'

This is clearly Josephus's 'root of Baaras' over again. Gerarde further holds it to be the identical mandragoras of the Greeks, and called Circaea because it was used by Circe for love-potions and enchantments. If this be so, then what was the 'moly' given to Odysseus by Hermes wherewith to counteract the charms of Circe? Was it a totally different plant, or was it merely the same applied on the homœopathic principle? Mr. Andrew Lang thinks they cannot be the same, because the 'moly' is described by Homer as having a black root and a white flower, while the mandragoras is described by Pliny as having a yellow flower and white, fleshy roots. But we know that Homer is somewhat confusing in the matter of colours, and it is possible that various shades of the purplish flower of the true mandrake might appear to one observer as white, and to another as yellow. Upon the whole, the probability is that the two names meant one and the same plant, for the characteristics are too peculiar to be alike possessed by different species. If the moly were not mandragoras there is nothing else known to modern botany that it could be, unless it were rue, with which some scholars have sought to identify it, but not very successfully.

The learned author of Pseudosia Epidemica, or Vulgar Errors, at any rate, was clearly of opinion that moly and mandragoras were one and the same. He quotes also from Pliny that the ancient way of pulling the root was to get on the windward side of the plant, and with a sword to describe three circles about it, whilst the operator kept his face turned to the west. The dangers attending the plucking of mandrakes are shrewdly disposed of by Sir Thomas Browne with the remark that it is 'derogatory unto the Providence of God ... to impose so destructive a quality on any plant ...

whose parts are usefull unto many.' The same author mentions the superstition that the mandrake grows under gallows, fructified by the decaying bodies of criminals, that it grows both male and female, and that it shrieks upon eradication. This last idea he derides as 'false below confute, arising perhaps from a small and stridulous noise which, being firmly rooted, it maketh upon divulsion of parts.' 'A slender foundation,' he remarks, 'for such a vast conception; for such a noise we sometimes observe in other plants—in parsnips, liquorish, eringium, flags, and others.'

The belief that the root of the mandrake resembles the human figure is characterized by the writer last quoted, as a 'conceit not to be made out by ordinary inspection, or any other eyes than such as regarding the clouds behold them in shapes conformable to pre-apprehensions.' It is traceable to the bifurcation of the root; a formation, however, which is frequently found 'in carrots, parsnips, briony, and many others.' There is no other importance, therefore, to be attached to 'the epithet of Pythagoras, who calls it anthropomorphon, and that of Columella, who terms it semihomo;' nor to Albertus, 'when he affirmed that mandrakes represent mankind with the distinction of either sex.' The roots, which were commonly sold in various parts of Europe 'unto ignorant people, handsomely made out the shape of man or woman. But these are not productions of nature but contrivances of art, as divers have noted.... This is vain and fabulous, which ignorant people and simple women believe; for the roots which are carried about by impostors are made of the roots of canes, briony, and other plants.' And the method of manufacture is then explained by the erudite doctor. It is evident from what has been cited that the prevalence of the superstition, and the existence of the German *erdmann*, were matters of common knowledge in the latter half of the seventeenth century.

But the superstition can be traced still later, for as recently as 1810 some of these root-images were to be seen on sale in certain parts of France, and were purchased as love-charms. It is said that even now at this very day bits of the *Mandragoras officinalis* are worn by the young men and maidens of Greece to bring them fortune in their love-affairs.

In some parts of England—viz., in Oxfordshire, Buckinghamshire, and Somersetshire—the briony is called mandrake, and a small portion of the root is frequently given to horses among their food to make them sleek and improve their condition, and it is still also sold 'for medicinal and other purposes.' Yet in other places it is called 'Devil's Food,' because Satan is supposed to be perpetually watching over it and to jealously guard its magical properties. It is partly on this account, and partly because of its supposed effect in stimulating the passions, that the Arabs sometimes call the mandrake Tuphacel-sheitan, or Devil's Apple, although it is otherwise known as the Stone Apple. In many parts of Europe the mandrake is believed to possess, in common with some other plants, the power of opening locks and unshoeing horses.

The belief that the mandrake had some peculiar association with the devil has made it a favourite plant with sorcerers and workers of enchantment in all ages. Lord Bacon refers to it as a favourite in his time, 'whereof witches and impostors make an ugly image, giving it the form of a face at the top of the root,' and leaving the natural threads of the root 'to make a broad beard down to the foot.' Mr. Moncure Conway, however, says that the superstition rightly belonging to the mandrake was often transferred to other roots—probably in ignorance as to the identity of the real plant.

'Thus,' he says, 'the author of Secrets du Petit Albert says that a peasant had a bryonia root of human shape, which he received from a gipsy. He buried it at a lucky conjunction of the moon with Venus' (the reader will not fail to note the reference to the Goddess of Love) 'in spring, and on a Monday, in a grave, and then sprinkled it with milk in which three field-mice had been drowned. In a month it became more humanlike than ever. Then he placed it in an oven with vervain, wrapped it afterwards in a dead man's shroud, and so long as he kept it he never failed in luck at games or work.'

Then we learn from the same author that a German horse-dealer, of Augsburg, once lost a horse, and being poor, wandered in despair to an inn. There some men gave him a mandrake, and on his return home he found a bag of ducats on the table. His wife, however, did not like the business, and persuaded the man to return to give back the root to those from whom he got it. But he could not find the men again, and soon after the house was burned down, and both horse-dealer and wife perished.

The only suggestion from this story is that the mandrake was supposed to bring 'devil's luck,' although, if so, it is difficult to understand why the *erdmanns* were so carefully preserved from generation to generation. One German writer, Rist, says that he has seen one more than a century old, which had been kept in a coffin, on which was a cloth bearing a picture of a thief on the gallows and a mandrake growing underneath.

Coles, who wrote The Art of Simpling, in 1656, says the witches use the mandrake-roots, 'according to some, or, as I rather suppose, the roots of briony, which simple people take for the true mandrake, and make thereof an ugly image, by which they represent the person on whom they intend to exercise their witchcraft.' But their professions must at times have been even larger, for it is on record that a witch was executed near Orleans, in France, about 1605, who was charged with having kept a living mandrake-fiend, having the form of a female ape!

So much for the mandrake, of which, however, a good deal more might be said. But what has been said serves to establish that it was identical with the mandragora, and with the mandragoras of the Greeks; that it was probably also the briony; that superstitions have attached to it in all countries and from time immemorial, which ascribed to it occult virtues; that the powers it exercised varied a good deal according to locality and time, but that two main conceptions have almost universally prevailed, viz., that it was a stimulant, and a potent instrument in affairs of the heart.

What, then, is the Soma, or Homa, of the Hindu mythology—the ambrosia of the Indian gods? It has been the subject of much discussion and some difference among comparative mythologists. Soma was the chief deity among the ancient Hindus—the author of life, the giver of health, the protector of the weak, and the guide to immortality. Once he took upon himself the form of man, but was slain by men and braised in a mortar. The similarity with the Christian legend is remarkable, and the method of death should be borne in mind. After his death, Soma rose in flame to heaven, 'to be the benefactor of the world and the mediator between God and man.'

One of the articles of faith with the Hindus, therefore, is that they must hold communion with Soma, and they are taught thus to pray to him: 'O Soma! thou art the strength of our heroes and the death of our enemies, invincible in war! Fulfil our vows in battle, fight for us! None can resist thee; give us superiority! O Soma immortal! May we drink to thee and be immortal like thee!' Mr. Baring-Gould says that the whole legend of Soma is but the allegorical history of the plant *Sarcostemma viminalis*, which is associated with passionate love 'because of the intoxicating liquor which is derived from its juice. It is regarded as a godsend. The way in which it is prepared is by crushing it in a mortar; the juice is then thrown on the sacrificial flame and so rises to heaven.' The same writer tells us that a similar worship prevailed among the Iranians, who called the juice Homa, but they did not ferment it, and although they ascribed to it divine attributes, they did not make Homa a supreme deity. But both with them and with the Hindus, 'the partaking of the juice was regarded as a sacramental act, by virtue of which the receiver was embued with a portion of the divine nature.'

Another writer, the author of Bible Folklore, says that the 'old Soma was the same as the Persian Homa, a brilliant god, who gives sons to heroes, and husbands to maidens. The juice of the plant, pounded in an iron mortar, is greenish in colour, and is strained through a cloth and mixed with the sap of a pomegranate branch; the yellow juice is then strained through a vessel with nine holes. Among the Parsees it is drunk, not as by the Brahmins in large quantities by sixteen priests, but in small quantities by the two chief priests, and is thus not intoxicating.'

The symbol is confused with the deity, and 'Soma is at once the life-giving spring of the juice of immortality, and the juice itself'—a confusion not without analogy in some of the superstitions narrated of the mandrake. But of old Soma was drunk as mead was drunk by the Scandinavians, before and after battle. It gave power and good fortune as well as light and happiness, and when elevated into a god was supposed to be the origin of all creation.

Now, of the *Sarcostemma* it is to be noted that it belongs to the family of *Asclepiadaceæ*, which have all something more or less 'fleshy' looking about some parts of them, which, like the *Apocyneæ*, were in the old world credited with medicinal properties, and which are generally acrid, stimulating, and astringent. There are many poisonous members of the family, such as the dog's-bane and wolf's-bane of our own country, favourite plants with the enchanters, while the cowplant of Ceylon is of the same species.

In Garrett's Dictionary of India it is stated that the Soma of the Vedas is no longer known in India, and the same statement is repeated by many writers. It is certainly not indubitable that the *Sarcostemma viminalis* was the plant of wondrous virtues that was deified. On the other hand, we find that these ascribed virtues closely resemble those attributed to the mandrake, and it is known that the Aryan people received many of their ideas and superstitions from the old Jewish tribes.

We have seen, further, that belief in the peculiar power of the mandrake in certain directions was a settled belief at a very early period of the Jewish history, and we thus arrive at the very probable suggestion that the original Soma was neither more nor less than the mandrake of Reuben, the 'Baaras root' of Josephus, the mandragoras of the Greeks, the moly of Homer, the mandragora of Shakespeare, the mandragen of Germany, and the mandrake, again, of England.

CHAPTER VI.

THE SEA AND ITS LEGENDS.

ONE of the oldest superstitions connected with the sea is undoubtedly that which associated peril with the malefic influence of some individual on shipboard. We find it in the case of the seamen of Joppa, who, when overtaken by a 'mighty tempest' on the voyage to Tarshish, said to each other, 'Come and let us cast lots, that we may know for whose cause this evil is cast upon us.' The lot, as we know, fell upon Jonah, and after some vain wrestling with the inevitable, the men at last 'took up Jonah and cast him forth into the sea, and the sea ceased from her raging.'

Without offering here any comment on, or explanation of, the Scriptural narrative, let us compare it with the following remarkable story, which that indefatigable delver after old-world wonders, Charles Kirkpatrick Sharpe, reproduced.

Somewhere about midsummer of the year 1480, a ship, sailing out of the Forth for a port in Holland, was assailed by a furious tempest, which increased to such a remarkable degree for the mild season of the year, that the sailors were overcome with fear, and gave themselves up for lost. At length an old woman, who was a passenger by the vessel, came on deck and entreated them to throw her overboard as the only means of preserving their own lives, saying that she had long been haunted by an 'incubus' in the shape of a man, from whose grasp she could not free herself. Fortunately for all parties there was another passenger on board—a priest—who was called to the rescue. After a long admonition, and many sighs and prayers, 'there issued forth of the pumpe of the ship,' says Hollinshed, 'a foul and evil-favoured blacke cloud, with a mightie terrible noise, flame, smoke, and stinke, which presentlie fell into the sea, and suddenlie, thereupon, the tempest ceassed, and the ship passing in great quiet the residue of her journie, arrived in safetie at the place whither she was bound.'

There is doubtless some association between this class of superstition and the old Talmudic legend, according to which the devils were specially angered when, at the creation, man received dominion over the things of the sea. This was a realm of unrest and tempest, which the devils claimed as belonging to themselves. But, says the legend, although denied control of the life that is in the sea, the devils were permitted a large degree of power over its waters, while over the winds their rule was supreme.

There is scarcely a current legend or superstition which cannot be traced to very remote sources. Thus, in the Chaldæo-Babylonian cosmogony there was a Triad which ruled the three zones of the universe: the heaven, by Anu; the surface of the earth and the atmosphere, by Bel; and the underworld, by Nonah. Now, Nonah is held to be both the same as the Assyrian Hea, or Saviour, and as the Noah of the Bible. So when Tiamat, the dragon, or leviathan, opens 'the fountains of the great deep,' and Anu, 'the windows of heaven,' it is Hea, or Noah, who saves the life of man.

This legend is supposed by M. François Lenormant to explain an allusion in one of the most ancient Accadian manuscripts in the British Museum to 'the serpent of seven heads, that beats the sea.' This Hydra was the type of the destructive water-demon who figures in the legends of all countries.

In the same way, to the Syrian fish deities, Dagon and Artergatis, must we look for the origin of our Undines and fish-maidens, and mermaidens.

The 'Nixy' of Germany has by some been supposed traceable to 'Old Nick'; but this is not probable, since St. Nicholas has been the patron-saint of sailors for many centuries. It was during the time of the Crusades that a vessel on the way to the Holy Land was in great peril, and St. Nicholas assuaged a tempest by his prayers. Since then he has been supposed to be the protector of mariners, even as Neptune was in ancient times; and in most Roman Catholic countries you will find in seaport towns churches dedicated to St. Nicholas, to which sailors resort to return thanks for preservation at sea, and to make votive offerings.

The German Nixy was, no doubt, a later form of the old Norse water-god Nikke. You meet with him again, in another form, in Neckan, the soulless, of whom Matthew Arnold sings:

'In summer on the headlands
The Baltic sea along
Sits Neckan with his harp of gold,
And sings his plaintive song.'

The 'Nixa' along the Baltic coast was once, however, much feared by the fishermen. It was the same spirit which appears as the Kelpie in Scotland— a water-demon which caused sudden floods to carry away the unwary, and then devoured them.

There was a river-goddess in Germany, whose temple stood at Magdeburg, of whom a legend exists that she also once visited earth and went to market in a Christian costume, where she was detected by a continual dripping of water from the corner of her apron. Generally speaking, however, the Nixies may be described as the descendants of the Naiads of ancient times, and as somewhat resembling the Russian Rusalkas, of which the peasantry live in much dread.

A Russian peasant, it is said, is so afraid of the water-spirits that he will not bathe without a cross round his neck, nor ford a stream on horseback without signing a cross on the water with a scythe or knife. In some parts these water-spirits are supposed to be the transformed souls of Pharaoh and his host, when they were drowned, and the number is always being increased by the souls of those who drown themselves.

It is said that 'in Bohemia' fishermen have been known to refuse aid to drowning persons lest 'Vodyany' would be offended and prevent the fish from entering the nets.

This 'Vodyany,' however, seems rather a variant of the old Hydra, who reappears in the diabolical names so frequently given to boiling springs and dangerous torrents. The 'Devil's Tea-kettles' and 'Devil's Punch-bowls' of England and America have the same association as the weird legends connected with the Strudel and Wirbel whirlpools of the Danube, and with the rapids of the Rhine, and other rivers. Curiously enough, we find the same idea in The Arabian Nights, when 'The sea became troubled before them, and there arose from it a black pillar ascending towards the sky, and approaching the meadow, and behold it was a Jinn of gigantic stature.'

This demon was a waterspout, and waterspouts in China are attributed to the battles of dragons. 'The Chinese,' says Mr. Moncure Conway, 'have canonised of recent times a special protectress against the storm-demons of the coast, in obedience to the wishes of the sailors.'

The swan-maidens, who figure in so many legends, are mere varieties of the mer-maiden, and, according to the Icelandic superstition, they and all fairies were children of Eve, whom she hid away on one occasion when the Lord came to visit her, because they were not washed and presentable! They were, therefore, condemned to be invisible for ever.

A Scotch story, quoted by Mr. Moncure Conway, rather bears against this theory. One day, it seems, as a fisherman sat reading his Bible, a beautiful nymph, lightly clad in green, came to him out of the sea, and asked if the book contained any promise of mercy for her. He replied that it contained an offer of salvation to 'all the children of Adam,' whereupon she fled away with a loud shriek, and disappeared in the sea. But the beautiful stories of water-nymphs, of Undines and Loreleis, and mer-women, are too numerous to be even mentioned, and too beautiful, in many cases, to make one care to analyze.

There is a tradition in Holland that when, in 1440, the dikes were broken down by a violent tempest, the sea overflowed the meadows. Some women of the town of Edam, going one day in a boat to milk their cows, discovered a mermaid in shallow water floundering about with her tail in the mud. They took her into the boat, brought her to Edam, dressed her in women's clothes, and taught her to spin, and to eat as they did. They even taught her something of religion, or, at any rate, to bow reverently when she passed a crucifix; but they could not teach her to speak. What was the ultimate fate of this remarkable creature is not disclosed.

Everybody, of course, is familiar with the old sea-legend of the *Flying Dutchman*, whether in stories of phantom ships, or in the opera of Wagner. The spirit of Vanderdecken, which is still supposed to roam the waters, is merely the modern version of our old friend, Nikke, the Norwegian water-demon. This is a deathless legend, and used to be as devoutly believed in as the existence of Mother Carey, sitting away up in the north, despatching her 'chickens' in all directions to work destruction for poor Jack. But Mother Carey really turns out on inquiry to be a most estimable being, as we shall presently see.

'Sailors,' says Brand, in his Popular Antiquities, 'usually the boldest Men alive, are yet frequently the very abject slaves of superstitious Fear. They have various puerile Apprehensions concerning Whistling on Shipboard, carrying a Corpse, etc., all which are Vestiges of the old Woman in human Nature, and can only be erased by the united Efforts of Philosophy and Religion.'

It is to be regretted, however, that the good Brand did not devote as much attention to the superstitions of sailors as he did to those of some other folks.

As is the case with almost all folk-lore, little variety is to be found in the sea superstitions of different nations. The ideas of the supernatural on shipboard are pretty much the same, whether the flag flown be the Union Jack, the German Eagle, the French Tricolor, the American Stars and Stripes, or even the Chinese Dragon. These superstitions are numerous, and are tenaciously preserved, but yet it would not be fair to say that seamen are, as a class, more superstitious than landsmen of their own rank. The great mystery of the sea; the uncertainty of life upon its bosom; the isolation and frequent loneliness; the wonder of the storms, and calms, and lights—everything connected with a sailor's occupation is calculated to impress him with the significance of signs and omens.

That mariners do not like to have a corpse on board is not remarkable, for many people ashore get rather 'creepy' if they have to sleep in a house where lies a dead body. Moreover, the old idea of bad luck which led to the throwing overboard of Jonah, is in this case transferred from the living to the dead. The objection to whistling is also explainable by the time-honoured practice of 'whistling for a wind,' for an injudicious whistler might easily bring down a blow from the wrong quarter.

There are some animals and birds which have a peculiar significance at sea. The cat, for instance, is generally disliked, and many sailors will not have one on board at any price. If there is one which becomes unusually frisky, they will say the cat has got a gale of wind in her tail. On one part of the Yorkshire coast, it is said, sailors' wives were in the habit of keeping black cats to insure the safety of their husbands at sea, until black cats became so scarce and dear that few could afford to buy one. Although Jack does not like a cat in the ship, he will not throw one overboard, for that would bring on a storm.

Miss L. A. Smith, in her book about the Music of the Waters, states that a dead hare on a ship is considered a sign of an approaching hurricane; and Cornish fishermen declare that a white hare seen about the quays at night indicates that there will be rough weather.

The pig is an object of aversion to Japanese seamen, and also to Filey fishermen, who will not go to sea if they meet one in the early morning. But, indeed, the pig seems to be generally disliked by all seafarers—except in the form of salt pork and bacon.

Rats, however, are not objected to; indeed, it would be useless to object, for they overrun all ships. And rats are supposed to leave a vessel only when it is going to sink. A Welsh skipper, however, once cleared his ship of them without the risk of a watery grave, by drawing her up to a cheese-laden ship in harbour. He quietly moored alongside, and, having left the hatches open all night, cast off with a chuckle in the morning, leaving a liberal legacy to his neighbour.

The stormy petrel is supposed to herald bad weather, and the great auk to tell that land is very near. This is true enough as regards the auk, which never ventures beyond soundings; but one doubts the truth of the popular belief that when the sea-gulls hover near the shore, a storm is at hand. The Scotch rhyme runs:

'Seagull, seagull, sit on the sand;
It's never good weather when you're on the land!'

Mr. Thiselton-Dyer quotes from Sinclair's Statistical Account of Scotland, in confirmation of this belief, that in the county of Forfar, 'when they appear in the fields, a storm from the southeast generally follows; and when the storm begins to abate, they fly back to the shore.' This does not accord with the present writer's experience of the west coast of Scotland, where the sea-gulls frequent the lochs and hillsides far inland all the summer. Naturally there are storms sometimes after their appearance, but just as often fine weather continues. As well say that the flocks of these beautiful birds that follow in the wake of a tourist steamer, to pick up unconsidered trifles, presage sea-sickness to the passengers!

One has heard that in Cornwall sailors will not walk at night along portions of the shore where there have been many wrecks, because they believe that the souls of the drowned haunt such localities, and that the 'calling of the dead' is frequently audible. Some even say that they have heard the voices of dead sailors hailing them by name. One can readily excuse a timorousness in Jack in such circumstances. Many persons besides sailors shrink from localities which have been the scenes of murder or sudden death.

Friday is the sailor's pet aversion, as an unlucky day on which to sail or begin work. But this is not surprising, when we remember that Friday has everywhere more superstition and folk-lore attached to it than any other day in the week, originating, perhaps, as Mr. Thiselton-Dyer suggests, from the fact that it was the day on which Christ was crucified. Lord Byron had the superstitious aversion to Friday; and even among the Brahmins no business must be commenced on this day. In Lancashire a man will not 'go a-courting on Friday'; and Brand says: 'A respectable merchant of the city of London informed me that no person will begin any business, that is, open his shop for the first time, on a Friday.' The 'respectable merchant' might be hard to find nowadays, but still one does not need to go to sailors to find a prejudice against Friday.

Other things which are accounted unlucky by superstitious seamen are: to sneeze on the left side at the moment of embarking; to count the men on board; to ask fishermen, before they start, where they are bound for; to point with the finger to a ship when at sea; to lose a mop or water-bucket; to cut the hair or nails at sea, except during a storm.

These are a few of the sea superstitions as preserved in rhyme:

'The evening gray, and the morning red,
Put on your hat or you'll wet your head.'

(Meaning that it will rain.)

'When the wind shifts against the sun,
Trust it not, for it will run.'

(That is, soon change again.)

'When the sun sets in the clear,
An easterly wind you need not fear.

'The evening red and morning gray
Are sure signs of a fine day.'

(A distich not peculiar to followers of the sea.)

'But the evening gray and morning red
Makes the sailor shake his head.'

This refers to the barometer:

'First rise, after low,
Indicates a stronger blow.'

And this:

'Long foretold, long last;
Short notice, soon past.'

These, however, are hardly superstitions, but maxims based on experience. Of the same character are the following:

'In squalls
When the rain's before the wind
Halyards, sheets, and braces mind.'

Also,

'When the wind's before the rain
Soon you may make sail again.'

And

'When the glass falls low,
Prepare for a blow;
When it rises high,
Let all your kites fly.

'A rainbow in the morning,
Sailors take warning;
A rainbow at night
Is the sailor's delight.'

The Manx fishermen have some curious sayings about herrings. Thus the common expression, 'As dead as a herring,' is due to them. They say also, 'Every herring must hang by its own gills'; and their favourite toast is, 'Life to man and death to fish.' They count one hundred and twenty-four fish to the hundred, thus: they first sort out lots of one hundred and twenty, then add three to each lot, which is called 'warp,' and then a single herring, which is called 'tally.' Before shooting the nets at sea, every man goes down on his knees at a sign from the skipper of the boat, and, with his head uncovered, prays for a blessing on the fishing. This, at least, used to be the general practice, but in how prevailing at the present day is doubtful.

The sound of the death-bell is often supposed to be heard at sea before a wreck, and this idea may be either associated with the bell-buoy which marks many sunken, dangerous rocks, or with the religious ceremonies of the old days.

At Malta it is, or was, usual to ring the church bells for an hour during a storm 'that the wind may cease and the sea be calmed,' and the same custom prevails both in Sicily and Sardinia.

A Cornish legend of the bells of a church, which were sent by ship that was lost in sight of the town, owing to the blasphemy of the captain, says that the bells are supposed to be in the bay, and they announce by strange sounds the approach of a storm.

There is a suggestion of Sir Ralph the Rover in this legend; but, indeed, the superstitions of those connected with the sea are so interwoven, that it is not easy to disentangle them, and they are numerous enough to need a book to themselves. No doubt our mariners derived many of them from the old Spanish navigators who once swayed the main, for the Spaniards are one of the most superstitious peoples in the world.

CHAPTER VII.

MOTHER CAREY AND HER CHICKENS.

WHO was Mother Carey the appearance of whose 'chickens' is supposed by the mariner to foretell a coming storm? This question is often asked, but seldom answered, and so a little light on the subject is desirable.

Charles Kingsley gives a very vivid picture of her. In his charming book about The Water-Babies, he tells how little Tom, in search of his old master, Grimes, is instructed to find his way to Peacepool and Mother Carey's Haven, where the good whales go when they die. On his way he meets a flock of petrels, who invite him to go with them, saying: 'We are Mother Carey's own chickens, and she sends us out over all the seas to show the good birds the way home.' So he comes to Peacepool at last, which is miles and miles across; and there the air is clear and transparent, and the water calm and lovely; and there the good whales rest in happy sleep upon the slumbering sea.

In the midst of Peacepool was one large peaked iceberg. 'When Tom came near it, it took the form of the grandest old lady he had ever seen—a white marble lady, sitting on a white marble throne. And from the foot of the throne there swam away, out and in, and into the sea, millions of new-born creatures, of more shapes and colours than man ever dreamed. And they were Mother Carey's chickens, whom she makes out of the sea-water all the day long.'

Now, this beautiful fancy of Kingsley's—and how beautiful it is can only be realized by a reading of the whole story—is based upon fact, as all beautiful fancies must be.

The fundamental idea of Kingsley's picture is that of a fruitful and beneficent mother. And Mother Carey is just the Mater Cara of the medieval sailors. Our Mother Carey's chickens are the 'Birds of the Holy Virgin,' of the South of Europe, the 'Oiseaux de Nôtre Dame' of the French seamen.

One reason for associating the petrel with the Holy Mother may possibly have been found in its supposed sleeplessness. The bird was believed never to rest, to hatch its eggs under its wings, and to be incessantly flying to and fro on the face of the waters on messages of warning to mariners. Even to this day sailors believe that the albatross, the aristocratic relative of the petrel, sleeps on the wing; and the power of the albatross, for good and evil, readers of the Ancient Mariner will remember. We say for good and evil, because opinion fluctuated. Thus:

'At length did cross an albatross,
Through the fog it came;
As if it had been a Christian soul,
We hailed it in God's name.'

When the mariner with his crossbow did shoot the albatross, the crew said:

'I had done a hellish thing,
And it would work them woe;
For all averred I had killed the bird
That made the breeze to blow.
"Ah, wretch!" said they, "the bird to slay,
That made the breeze to blow!"'

And once more, when the weather cleared, they changed:

'Then all averred I had killed the bird
That brought the fog and mist;
"'Twas right," said they, "such birds to slay,
That bring the fog and mist!"'

Coleridge got his idea from Wordsworth, who got it from a passage in Shelvocke's voyages, where a long spell of bad weather was attributed to an albatross following the ship.

The poet who sang,

'Oh, stormy, stormy peterel!
Thou art a bird of woe,
Yet would I thou could'st tell me half
Of the misery thou dost know!'

has, however, misunderstood the feeling with which that little harbinger is regarded. So have many other persons. The petrel is not a bird of woe, but a bird of warning.

The Virgin Mary—Mater Cara—was the special protectress of the early Christian seamen, just as Amphitrite had been the tutelary genius of his Greek, and Venus of his Roman, progenitors, and just as Isis, the moon goddess, had been the patroness of the Egyptian navigators. The Catholic mariner still believes that the Virgin has especial power over the winds and the sea.

At Marseilles is the shrine of the Nôtre Dame de la Garde, greatly venerated by all the Provençal sailors; at Caen is the shrine of Nôtre Dame de Deliverance; at Havre, that of Nôtre Dame des Neiges. Brand tells, in his book of Antiquities, that on Good Friday Catholic mariners 'cock-bill' their yards in mourning and hang and scourge an effigy of Judas Iscariot. The practice still continues, and as recently as 1881 a London newspaper contained an account of the ceremony performed on board several Portuguese vessels in the London Docks. The proceedings always closed with a Hymn to the Virgin Mary.

In Rome, at the Church of Santa Maria della Navicella, there is a small marble ship which was offered by Pope Leo the Tenth in execution of a vow after his escape from shipwreck. The first thing done by Magellan and his crew after their safe return to Seville was to perform penance barefooted, clad only in their shirts, and bearing lighted tapers in their hands, at the shrine of Our Lady of Victory. And it is related of Columbus, that on safe arrival after a storm at the Azores, 'The Admiral and all the crew, bearing in remembrance the vow which they had made the Thursday before, to go barefooted, and in their shirts, to some church of Our Lady at the first land, were of opinion that they ought to discharge this vow. They accordingly landed, and proceeded, according to their vow, barefooted, and in their shirts, toward the hermitage.'

Countless instances might be cited, but these will suffice to show the estimation in which Mater Cara was held by Catholic seamen.

How it came to be supposed that the smaller *Procellariæ* are only visible before a storm is not very apparent. In point of fact, there is no more reason for associating the petrel specially with storms than there is for the belief expressed in the old Scotch couplet quoted in the last chapter:

'Seagull, seagull, sit in the sand;
It's never good weather when you're on the land!'

As a matter of fact, seagulls do fly far inland in fine weather, and especially during ploughing-time. And also, as a matter of fact, the petrel lives at sea both in fine weather and foul, because he is uncomfortable on land. It is only the breeding season that he spends on shore; while the seagull is just as much at home on the land as on the sea.

The scientific name of the petrel tribe is *Procellariæ*, from the Latin *procella*—a storm. It is a large family, all the members of which are distinguished by a peculiar tube-like arrangement of the nostrils. Their feet, also, are peculiar in being without any back toe, so that they can only with great difficulty rise on the wing from dry land.

Mother Carey's chickens are among the smaller species of this family, and they have both a shorter bill and a longer leg than their relatives. But all the *Procellariæ* are noted for ranging further from land than any other of the sea-birds. Thus they are often visible from ship-board when no other animal life can be sighted; and thus it was, doubtless, that their appearance suggested safe harbour, and consequent thanks to Mater Cara, to the devout seaman.

Why the petrels are associated with storms is thus not easily explained, seeing that they are abroad in all weathers; but a feasible suggestion was advanced by Pennant. It is that they gather from the water sea-animals which are most abundant before or after a storm, when the sea is in a state of unusual commotion. All birds are highly sensitive to atmospheric changes, and all sea-birds seem to develop extra activity in threatening and 'dirty' weather.

There is another interesting thing about Mother Carey's chicken, and that is, that he is also called petrel, from the Italian 'Petrello,' or Little Peter. This is because he is supposed to be able, like the apostle, to walk on the water, and as in fact he does after a fashion, with the aid of his wings.

Now, St. Peter, both as a fisherman and for his sea-walking, was always a favourite saint with sailors, and was often invoked during storms. He was the patron saint of Cortez, as he was also of the Thames watermen. There is an old legend that St. Peter went on board a fisherman's boat somewhere about the Nore, and that it carried him, without sails or oars, to the very spot which he selected as the site for Westminster Abbey.

In the Russian ports of the Baltic there is firm belief in a species of water-spirits called Rusalkas, who raise storms and cause much damage to the shipping. The great anniversary of these storm-spirits is St. Peter's Day. The John Dory is St. Peter's fish, and it is said that the spots on each side of its mouth are the marks of the apostle's thumb and forefinger. It was called 'janitore,' or doorkeeper, because in its mouth was found the penny with which the temple-tax was paid. Now, St. Peter also was the doorkeeper of heaven, and from janitore to John Dory was an easy transition.

With fishermen, as was natural, St. Peter was held in high honour; and in Cornwall and Yorkshire, until recently, it was customary to light bonfires, and to hold other ceremonies, on St. Peter's Day, to signalize the opening of the fishing season, and to bespeak luck. An old writer says of these customs at Guisboro', in Yorkshire, that:

'The fishermen, on St. Peter's daye, invited their friends and kinfolk to a festivall kept after their fashion, with a free hearte, and no show of niggardnesse. That day their boats are dressed curiously for the showe, their masts are painted, and certain rytes observed amongst them with sprinkling their bows with good liquor, which custome or superstition, sucked from their ancestors, even continueth down unto this present tyme.'

Perhaps at 'this present tyme' the ceremonies are not so elaborate; but survivals of the 'custome or superstition' are to be found yet in our fishing villages.

It is probable that the observers of St. Peter's Day do not know the origin of their curious customs. It is certain that sailors, as a class, do not now know why their favourite little bird is called petrel. We have tried to remove the stigma which in modern times has come to rest upon Mother Carey's chickens. Let us no longer do them wrong by supposing that they are always the harbingers of woe. They have a busy and a useful life, and it is one, as we have seen, with tender, even sacred, associations.

It may be recalled as an interesting, although not an agreeable item, that in the days of the French Revolution there was a notorious brood of Mother Carey's chickens in Paris. They were the female rag-tag-and-bobtail of the city, whose appearance in the streets was understood to forebode a fresh political tumult. What an insult to our feathered friends to bestow their honoured name on such human fiends!

The real Mother Carey is she who appeared to Tom and Ella in Peacepool, after they had learned a few things about themselves and the world. They heard her voice calling to them, and they looked, crying:

"'Oh, who are you, after all? You are our dear Mrs. Do-as-you-would-be-done-by.'"

"'No, you are good Mrs. Be-done-by-as-you-did; but you are grown quite beautiful now!'"

"'To you,' said the Fairy; 'but look again.'"

"'You are Mother Carey,' said Tom, in a very low, solemn voice, for he had found out something which made him very happy, and yet frightened him more than all that he had ever seen.

"'But you are grown quite young again.'"

"'To you,' said the Fairy; 'but look again.'"

'"You are the Irishwoman who met me the day I went to Harthover!"

'And when they looked again she was neither of them, and yet all of them at once.

'"My name is written in my eyes, if you have eyes to see it there."

'And they looked into her great, deep soft eyes, and they changed again and again into every hue, as the light changes in a diamond.

'"Now read my name," said she at last, and her eyes flashed for one moment, clear, white, blazing light; but the children could not read her name, for they were dazzled, and hid their faces in their hands.

'They were only water-babies, and just beginning to learn the meaning of love.'

CHAPTER VIII.

DAVY JONES'S LOCKER.

THIS expression of what may be called nautical slang has now become almost classic. At all events, everybody knows it; and most people may be presumed to know that to 'go to Davy Jones's Locker' is equivalent to 'losing the number of your mess,' or, as the Californian miners say, 'passing in your checks.' Being especially a sea-phrase, it means, of course, to be drowned. But how did the phrase originate? And who was Davy Jones? These questions must have frequently occurred to many, and it is worth while seeking an answer to them. There is an explanation for everything, if one only knows how to look for it.

This saying about Davy Jones is a very old one—so old, that it cannot possibly have any reference to the famous Paul Jones. In fact, one hears very often of 'Davy's Locker' without any reference to 'Jones' at all. Then 'Davy,' again, is a vulgar slang expression for affidavit, but it is also used in thief-parlance by way of an oath. 'So help me Davy!' is the slang equivalent for the concluding sentence of the oath administered in the police-courts with which these gentry are familiar. It has thus been inferred that 'Davy' is a slang expression of somewhat blasphemous import; but this is by no means certain.

It is much more likely to be associated with, or to have the same origin as, the 'Duffy' of the West Indian negroes. Among them Duffy means a ghost; and in the vocabulary of the gutter it may easily have been taken as the equivalent of soul. The transition from Duffy to Davy is by no means difficult.

But how, then, did the vagabond users of 'flash' language get hold of this word? It is probable enough that it was brought home by the sailors from the West Indies, and picked up at the docks by the waifs and strays of our vast vagrant population. On the other hand, it is just as likely that the West Indian negroes picked up 'Duffy' from our own sailors; and that, in fact, Duffy is just the nigger contraction of Davy Jones. There is certainly a very close connection, both in sound and meaning, between the two expressions.

We must go further back and further away, however, to get to the root of this matter. And, if we inquire diligently, we shall find our Davy in the Deva of the Indian mythology. The original Sanskrit meaning of Deva was 'The Shining One,' but in the operation of what has been called 'the degradation of Deities' in the Oriental religions, it became synonymous with our devil. In fact, we owe the word 'devil' to this same Sanskrit root; and it is noteworthy that while Deva meant the Good Spirit to the Brahmans, it meant the Evil Spirit to the Parsees. In this root we may also find the explanation of the gipsy word for God, which, curiously enough, is Devel.

While it is easy to trace the transition from Deva to the sailor's Davy, one may note another curious thing. The name of the fabulous Welshman, Taffy, the thief, is a corruption of Dyved, which, as signifying an evil spirit, is the Cymric form of Deva. This would almost suggest that the addition of the apparent surname, Jones, was a Welsh performance. But this is only an amusing conjecture, not without a certain aptness.

For the origin of Jones we must look to Jonah, who in nautical history is regarded as the embodiment of malevolence at sea. The prophet Jonah is not the only one who has been committed to the deep to appease the storm-fiends, whose anger his presence was supposed to have aroused. It is easy to account for this from the Bible narrative. 'The mariners were afraid, and cried every man unto his God. And they said, every one to his fellow, "Come, and let us cast lots, that we may know for whose cause this evil is upon us." So they cast lots, and the lot fell upon Jonah. So they took up Jonah and cast him forth into the sea, and the sea ceased from her raging.'

The superstition of sailors is proverbial, and to this day they believe in good or ill luck being brought to a vessel by persons and things. In olden times there were many sacrifices to this Jonah superstition; and even in comparatively recent times, Holcroft, the actor, on a voyage to Scotland, narrowly escaped a watery grave, because the men took him for 'the Jonas.' And to this day 'He's a Jonah' is an expression often enough heard on shipboard applied to some unwelcome passenger.

Here, then, we have the Sanskrit origin of Davy, and the Biblical origin of Jones, both words embodying much the same idea to the mind of the primitive seamen.

But what of the 'locker'?

This, of course, is a familiar piece of ship-furniture which it was not difficult to transfer to the mythical demon of the deep. Lieutenant Bassett thought that the locker might be the whale's belly in which Jonah found refuge; but this is hardly in harmony with the meaning of the phrase. In the sense in which it is thus used, locker does not mean a temporary resting-place or submarine harbour of refuge, but a place of final deposit. It is possible, indeed, to find the origin of the word locker as here applied in Loki, the personification of evil in the Scandinavian mythology. Loki, like

Deva, was not always an evil spirit, but he became eventually identified with Satan. He became a flame-demon, a sort of incarnate spirit of fire.

There is good reason for believing in this theory of the Scandinavian origin of the word 'locker' as used in the connection we are considering. It is to be remembered that, in olden times, death by drowning was even more dreaded than now, because drowned bodies were supposed to be debarred from the Resurrection. Going far back, we find that the sea was the abode of Typhœus, who, besides being a hurricane-raising, was also a fire-breathing, demon, and was feared as the quencher of the sun, who sank at night into his bosom. The legend of St. Brandan and his burning islands preserved the idea that Hades was very near to the bottom of the ocean. Thus, then, we may readily perceive the conception of Loki having his receptacle for drowned mariners in the bed of the sea. A belief prevailed long into the Middle Ages that the sea-bottom was the abode of many demons, who lay in wait for passengers, to drag them down to the infernal depths.

Thus, then, Davy Jones's Locker became, by a mixture of theogonies, 'the ocean, the deep sea-bottom, the place to which the body was committed, and to which the souls of the wicked fled.'

This meaning is now somewhat modified. Sailors do not, as Smollett says they did in his day, regard Davy Jones as the fiend who presides over all the evil spirits of the deep, and who is seen in various shapes, warning the devoted wretches of death and woe. In fact, it is not Davy Jones they think of at all now, but his Locker; for to go to Davy's Locker is to be lost at sea and to find a watery grave.

There is, however, a curious survival of the personal element still to be traced in some of the sailors' chanties. Take, for instance, that remarkable one about 'Burying the Dead Horse,' which still puzzles the passengers on board the packets sailing to the Antipodes. Without going into the question of the song and its attendant ceremonies just now, the following lines may be quoted as bearing on our subject:

'You poor old horse, what brought you here,
After carrying turf for many a year?
From Bantry Bay to Ballyack,
When you fell down and broke your back?
You died from blows and sore abuse,
And were salted down for the sailors' use.
The sailors they the meat despise;
They turned you over and —— your eyes;
They ate the meat and picked the bones,
And gave the rest to Davy Jones.'

All the offal of a ship is thrown over to Davy Jones—doubtless because there is nothing else to be done with it.

The favourite demon, if one may use the expression, of British sailors is now Old Nick, and one may trace his origin even more easily than that of Davy Jones. We can follow him through Saxon, German, Danish and Norwegian transitions to one of the names of Odin—Hnickar—for even All-father Odin shared the fate of his Oriental predecessors, and became demonized. Others, again, have carried the name Hnickar back still further to the Egyptian Nika, the serpent of the lower world, 'the Typhonic enemy of the Sun in his night-journey.'

It is to the same root that we owe the Necken of the Baltic, and the Nixies—the water-fays—of the German legends. It is to the Norwegian Nökke, also, that we owe the Wild Huntsman of the Sea, on which the story of the *Flying Dutchman* and a host of other legends of demon vessels and demon mariners are founded.

There is, however, some confusion in the nautical mythology between the original Old Nick and the popular Saint Nicholas. This saint became the Christian successor of Neptune, as the protector of seamen. 'This saintly Poseidon,' says Mr. Conway, 'the patron of fishermen, in time became associated with the demon whom the British sailor feared if he feared nothing else. He was also of old the patron of pirates; and robbers were called "St. Nicholas' clerks."'

It is certainly one of the curiosities of plutology that the patron saint of children who is still honoured at Christmas as Santa Claus should be the same as the dreaded Old Nick of the seafarers.

These investigations are extremely interesting, and may lead us far; but our present purpose is merely to find an explanation of a popular phrase.

It is more difficult to explain a number of other marine personalities, who are as lively to-day on shipboard as they were generations ago. There is, for instance, old Mister Storm-Along, of whom the chanty-man sings:

'When Stormy died, I dug his grave—
I dug his grave with a silver spade;
I hove him up with an iron crane,
And lowered him down with a golden chain.'

Who was he? And who was the famous Captain Cottington, of whom it is related, in stentorian tones and with tireless repetition, that:

'Captain Cottington, he went to sea,
Captain Cottington, he went to sea-e-e-e,
Captain Cottington, he went to sea,
Captain Cottington, he went to sea-e!'

Who, also, was 'Uncle Peleg,' of whom a somewhat similarly exhaustive history is chanted? And, still more, who was the mysterious Reuben Ranzo, with whose name every fo'cs'le of every outward-bound British or American ship is constantly resounding?

'Pity Reuben Ranzo—
Ranzo, boys, a Ranzo!
Oh, pity Reuben Ranzo—
Ranzo, boys, a Ranzo!'

He had a remarkable career, this Reuben, according to the song. He was a tailor by trade; went to school on the Monday, learnt to read on Tuesday, and by Friday he had thrashed the master. Then he went to sea, and, after some ignominious experiences, married the captain's daughter, and became himself the captain of a whaler. But who was he? And how does he come to exercise such a fascination over all mariners, even unto this day?

This is one of the mysteries of the ocean. The sea is covered with mystery, and with phantom shapes. Every ship that sails is peopled with a crew of dim shadows of the past that none can explain.

CHAPTER IX.

SOME FLOWERS OF FANCY.

THAT the lily should symbolize purity seems appropriate enough, but why should parsley in olden times have been associated with death? It is recorded that a few bundles of parsley once threw a whole Greek army into panic, because in Greece the tombs of the dead were strewn with the herb. With them 'to be in need of parsley' was equivalent to being beyond hope.

The name itself offers little explanation of this superstition, for it is derived from the Latin *petroselinum*, which, again, was taken from the Greek name signifying the 'plant of the rocks.' According to the myth, however, it sprang from the blood of Archemorus, or Orpheltes, the son of Lycurgus, King of Nemæa. Archemorus was killed by a serpent while his foster-mother was showing the soldiers of Adrastus where they might find a fountain. On the place where he died there sprang up the parsley, which the Greeks, in grief for his loss, wove into chaplets for the victors at the Nemæan games. At these games it was always customary to deliver a funeral oration in memory of Archemorus, while the participators were dressed in mourning. Hence the association of parsley with death among the Greeks, and the long-prevailing Western belief that the plant is 'unlucky,' is only another instance of the marvellous longevity of superstitions.

It is said by Mr. Thiselton-Dyer that in Devonshire to transplant parsley is accounted a serious offence against the tutelary spirit of the herb, and is certain to be punished within the year by some great misfortune. In South Hampshire the country people will never give parsley away, for fear of trouble; and in Suffolk it is believed that if it be sown on any other day than Good Friday it will not grow double. The *Folklore Record*, some years ago, gave the case of a gentleman near Southampton whose gardener refused to sow some parsley-seed when ordered, because 'it would be a bad day's work' for him to do so; the most he would do was to bring a plant or two, and throw them down for the master to pick up if he chose. To give them, however, the man regarded as fatal.

But even to move parsley is regarded in some places to be unlucky, and we have heard of a parish clerk in Devonshire who was bedridden, and who was popularly supposed to owe his trouble to having moved some parsley-beds. There is a similar superstition in Germany, and many readers have probably often come across an old saying, that 'Parsley fried will bring a man to his saddle and a woman to her grave.' The allusion to the saddle is obscure; but it is obvious that all the superstitious dread of parsley is a survival of the old Greek fable immortalized in the Nemæan games.

That the rose should be associated with death may appear strange to some, yet so it was. The Greeks certainly used the rose in their funeral rites and for the decoration of their tombs. The Romans used it for similar purposes, and often bequeathed legacies for the express purpose of keeping their tombs adorned with the flower. Whether it was by them that the practice was introduced into England is not capable of direct proof, but it is worthy of note that at Ockley, a place where the Romans were often located in large numbers, it was a custom of comparatively recent experience for girls to plant roses upon the graves of their dead lovers. Hence, no doubt, its origin in Gay's riddle:

'What flower is that which royal honour craves,
Adjoins the Virgin, and 'tis strewn on graves?'

The answer is 'Rosemary,' which, although sometimes understood to mean the Rose of the Virgin Mary, is neither a rose, nor is it in any special way associated with the Virgin.

On the other hand, the rose is associated by most Catholics with the Mother of the Saviour, and in Italy especially, during the celebrations of May, the rose is abundantly used. By some it has been thought that the early association of the rose with death led to the expression 'under the rose,' applied to anything to be done in secret or silence. Others, again, have ascribed the origin of that expression to the perfect beauty of the flower, which, as language is unable to portray it, may be a symbol of silence. Sir Thomas Browne, however, says the origin was either in the old custom of wearing chaplets of roses during the 'Symposiack meetings,' or else because the rose was the flower of Venus, 'which Cupid consecrated unto Harpocrates, the god of silence.' There is a basis of probability in both theories, and all know that the rose was peculiarly the property of the Goddess of Love. Indeed, according to the old fable, the flower was originally white until dyed by the blood which flowed from the foot of Venus, pierced by a thorn as she ran to the aid of her loved Adonis. Hence Spenser says:

'White as the native rose, before the change
Which Venus's blood did in her leaves impress.'

According to others, however, it was the blood of Adonis which dyed the flower. Thus Bion, in his Lament: 'A tear the Paphian sheds for each blood-drop of Adonis, and tears and blood on the earth are turned to flowers. The blood brings forth the rose, and the tears the wind-flower. Woe, woe, for Adonis! he hath perished, the lovely Adonis!' This tradition is preserved in the German name, *Adonis-blume*, which, however, is usually applied to the anemone.

The rose being the emblem of love, and love having a natural abhorrence of publicity, it is not difficult to conceive the connection with silence. It is said that the Romans used to place a decoration of roses in the centre of their dining-rooms, as a hint to the guests that all that was said at the banqueting-table was in the nature of 'privileged communications,' and in old Germany a similar custom long prevailed. In the sixteenth century a rose was placed over confessionals, and the inference is that the hint was then well understood.

There was also an obvious meaning in the adoption by the Jacobites of this flower as the emblem of the Pretender, to whose service they were secretly sworn. It was the white rose that was especially affected by the Stuarts, and the Pretender's birthday, the 10th of June, was for long known as 'White Rose Day,' much as 'Primrose Day' is now definitely associated with the late Lord Beaconsfield. The story of the Wars of the Roses is, of course, known to everybody, and how, in consequence of these feuds, the rose became the emblem of England, as the thistle is of Scotland, and the shamrock of Ireland.

In the East there is even more of poetic significance attached to the rose than with us. It is related of Sadi, the Persian poet, that, when a slave, he earned his freedom by the adroit use of the flower. One day he presented a rose to his master, with the remark, made with all humility, 'Do good to thy servant whilst thou hast the power, for the season of power is often as transient as the duration of this flower.' This was in allusion to the Eastern fancy, which makes the white rose the emblem of life—transient and uncertain. In Persia they have a festival called 'The Feast of the Roses,' which lasts during the blooming of the flowers. One of their great works is called The Garden of Roses, and in all their poems and tales they closely associate the rose with the bulbul or nightingale. The belief is that the bird derives his melody from the beauteous flower, and they say, 'You may place a handful of fragrant herbs and flowers before the nightingale, but he wants nothing more than the odour of his beloved rose.'

Thomas Moore seizes, with happy effect, on this legend in Lalla Rookh, which poem, indeed, is redolent of roses. But poetry generally is as full of the rose as the rose is of poetry, and it would take a volume to deal adequately with all the fancies and superstitious associations of the queen of flowers. Before quitting the subject, however, we should not overlook the Oriental traditions of how the rose received its various colours. It is said that when Mohammed was journeying to heaven, the sweat which fell from his forehead produced white roses, and that which fell from Al Borak produced yellow roses. But an older tradition is given by Sir John Mandeville. It is that of Zillah, the beauteous maiden of Bethlehem, who, being falsely accused, was condemned to be burned alive. At the stake the flames passed over her and shrivelled up her accuser, while, on the spot where she stood, sprang up a garden of roses—red where the fire had touched, and white where it had passed. 'And theise werein the first roseres that ever ony man saughe.'

Reference has been made to the lily as the emblem of purity, but, curiously enough, this innocent-looking flower has its baleful superstitions as well.

In Devonshire it is accounted unlucky to plant a bed of lilies-of-the-valley, and to do so is to ensure misfortune, if not death, within a year. Yet this flower has always been closely associated with the Virgin Mary, and according to one legend, it sprang from some of the milk which fell to the ground as she was nourishing the infant Jesus. The Greeks, however, had a similar legend, ascribing the origin of the flower to a drop of Juno's milk. The Greeks have always made a favourite of the lily, and even to this day use it largely in making up bridal wreaths, while the sacred significance which Christians have found in the flower may be traceable to our Lord's use of it in imagery.

In this connection the legend of the budding lily of St. Joseph may be recalled, and also the fact that the mediæval painters generally depicted the Madonna with a lily in her hand. There is a tradition that the lily was the principal ornament in the crown of Solomon, and that it typified love, charity, purity, and innocence—a combination of virtues hardly to be found in the character of the wise King himself.

Nor must we forget that the sacred flower of the East—the lotus—is a lily, and that even to name it seems to carry ineffable consolation to the Buddhist. Thus, the universal prayer of the Buddhists—that prayer which is printed on slips and fastened on cylinders which are incessantly revolving in Thibet—'Om mani padme hum!' means simply, 'Oh, the jewel in (or of) the lotus! Amen!' So Sir Edwin Arnold, in The Light of Asia:

'Ah, Lover! Brother! Guide! Lamp of the Law!
I take my refuge in Thy name and Thee!
I take my refuge in Thy Law of Good!
I take my refuge in Thy Order! Om!
The dew is on the lotus. Rise, Great Sun,
And lift my leaf, and mix me with the wave.
"Om mani padme hum," the sunrise comes.
The dewdrop slips into the shining sea!'

The lily, or lotus, was held sacred also in ancient Egypt, and the capitals of many of the buildings bear the form of an open lotus-flower. And naturally, in a land of Buddhism like China, the lotus occupies there an important place, both in art, in poetry, and in popular fancy. It is recorded that the old Jews regarded the lily, or lotus (*Lilium candidum*), as a protection against enchantment, and it is said that Judith wore a wreath of lilies when she went to visit Holofernes, by way of counteractant charm.

The lotus which is the sacred lily of the East must not be confounded with the mysterious plant mentioned by Ulysses, and of which Tennyson has sung—the plant of oblivion and sensuousness. That there is an element of enchantment about the lily we have seen is still believed in our own country, but the association of misfortune with it is not universal. On the contrary, in some parts the leaf of the lily is supposed to have curative virtues in cases of cuts and wounds, and Gerarde, the old herbalist, even says that 'the flowers of lily-of-the-valley, being close stopped up in a glass, put into an ant-hill, and taken away again a month after, ye shall find a liquor in the glass, which being outwardly applied, helpeth the gout.' One hears, perhaps, of no modern experiments having been made with this remedy. But if not to cure gout, the flower has, it appears, been used to pay rents, for Grimm says that some lands in Hesse were held upon the condition of presenting a bunch of lily-of-the-valley every year. This, of course, would not be the whole burden, and the custom had, no doubt, a religious origin and significance.

The flower is often associated with the sword of justice, and both the Dominicans and the Cistercians held it in high honour. It is worth noting, too, that some traditions make the lily the favourite flower of St. Cecilia, although the popular legend makes the angel bring her a bouquet of roses every night from Paradise.

But how did the lily become the badge of France? One tradition is that it was adopted by the French kings because it was the emblem of purity, and closely associated with both Christ and Solomon. One old legend has it that after one of the great battles of the Crusaders, the French banners were found covered with lilies. According to others, the Fleur de lys is merely a corruption of Fleur de Luce, or Fleur de Louis, and was not a lily at all, but the purple iris, which Louis the Seventh adopted for his emblem on his departure to the Holy Land. On the other hand, there is a legend that a shield of azure bearing the device of three golden lilies was presented by an angel to Clothilde, the wife of Clovis, and it is claimed that the lily has been the true national emblem of France ever since the time of that Sovereign. Whatever the origin, however, of Fleur de lys, it certainly means lily now, and the Lily of France is a symbol as definite as the Rose of England, as the Shamrock of Ireland, or as the Thistle of Scotland.

It is curious how much superstition and romance have clustered round the humble clover-leaf. Not one of us, perhaps, but has in childhood spent hours in looking for the four-leaved clover that was to bring untold luck. What trouble to find it! What joy when found! And what little profit beyond the joy of the search! As the old couplet has it, somewhat inconsequently:

'With a four-leav'd clover, double-topp'd ash, and green-topp'd seave,
You may go before the queen's daughter without asking leave.'

The advantage here suggested is not very obvious, but the Devonshire people had a more defined idea of the virtue of the double clover, and they state it thus:

'An even-leaved ash,
And a four-leaved clover;
You'll see your true lover
Before the day's over.'

But in Cambridgeshire it seems that the two-leaved clover is the object of desire, for there the saying goes:

'A clover, a clover of two,
Put it on your right shoe;
The first young man you meet,
In field, or lane, or street,
You shall have him,
Or one of his name.'

This, while presenting a considerable amount of uncertainty in the result has, at least, the merit of presaging something.

In other parts, however, and in more ancient days, the carrying of the four-bladed clover was believed to bring luck in play and in business, safety on a journey, and the power of detecting evil spirits. In Germany the clover was held almost sacred whenever it had two or four blades. Now, as to luck, a curious thing is stated by the author of the Plant Lore of Shakespeare. He says that clover is a corruption of *clava*, a club, and that to this day we preserve the emblem of luck on our playing-cards in painting the suit of clubs. Somehow the etymology does not seem very satisfying; but at any rate we all know what 'living in clover' means.

Yet, perhaps, everyone does not know that in rural districts the clover is looked upon as a capital barometer, the leaves becoming rough to the feel when a storm is impending. A writer, quoted by Mr. Thiselton-Dyer, says that when tempestuous weather is coming the clover will 'start and rise up as if it were afraid of an assault.'

It is probable that the association of good luck with the four-bladed clover arose from its fancied resemblance to the cross. Support is given to this hypothesis by the traditional origin of the shamrock as the badge of Ireland. In the account given of St. Patrick in The Book of Days, it is stated that once when the Saint wanted to illustrate the doctrine of the Trinity to his pagan hearers, he plucked a piece of the common white clover. Now, it seems that the trefoil is called *shamrakh* in Arabic, and was held sacred in Persia. And it is remarkable that Pliny says the trefoil is an antidote against the bites of snakes and scorpions. It is not by any means certain that the common clover was the original shamrock of Ireland; and even to this day many claim the title for the wood-sorrel. Still, for fifty years, at any rate, the popular belief has been that the trefoil-clover is the plant which was plucked by St. Patrick, who drove out the snakes from Ireland, who is still her patron-saint, and whose badge is worn to this day.

But how did the name come from Arabia, and what is the connection between Pliny's theory and the legend, of St. Patrick's victory over the vermin? These remain among the unsolved mysteries of folk-lore.

With the emblem of Scotland—the thistle—not so many classical associations and active superstitions are to be found, but yet it is not devoid of folk-lore. Of course opinions differ as to what was or is the true Scotch thistle, but of the several varieties of thistles many beliefs are entertained. One variety—the Carline—is esteemed in some parts as a barometer, as it closes up when rain is approaching. In Tartary there is a variety which grows to such a size that it is planted for shelter on the windward side of the huts on the Steppes. This thistle is called the 'Wind Witch,' because, after the heat of the summer is past, the dried portions take the form of a ball, with which the spirits are supposed to make merry in the autumnal gales.

The origin of the name thistle is probably Scandinavian, and associated with Thor. The plant was, at any rate, sacred to the Scandinavian god, and was believed by the old Vikings to receive the colour of the lightning into its blossom, which thereupon became endowed with high curative and protective virtues. There was a species of thistle on Dartmoor which used to be called Thormantle, and was used in that district as a febrifuge. Some writers have said that in Poland some infantile disorders are supposed to be the work of mischievous spirits using thistle-seed.

The Lady's Thistle, which some believe to be the true Scotch thistle, is one of the many plants associated with the Virgin. The tradition, according to Brand, is that the white spots on the leaves are due to the falling of some drops of the Holy Mother's milk, a legend we have seen to be attached also to the lily. Then the great Emperor Charlemagne's name is blended with that of the Carline Thistle, the story being that during the prevalence of an epidemic among his troops he prayed to God for help. An angel appeared, and indicated, by firing an arrow, a plant which would allay the disease. This was the *Carlina acaulis*, which, of course, cured all the sick soldiers, and possibly may have some of the febrifuge virtues which the Dartmoor people fancied existed in another kind of thistle. Nettle-soup is still a familiar housewife's remedy for some childish ailments.

In some parts of Germany there is a superstition that sores upon horses' backs may be cured by gathering four red thistle-blossoms before daybreak, and placing them in the form of a square upon the ground with a stone in the middle. It is not easy to trace the probable origin of this belief, but many of the old herbalists mention the thistle as efficacious in cases of vertigo, headache, jaundice, and 'infirmities of the gall.' Says one, 'It is an herb of Mars, and under the sign Aries.' Therefore, 'it strengthens the attractive faculty in man and clarifies the blood, because the one is ruled by Mars. The continual drinking the decoction of it helps red faces, tetters, and ringworms, because Mars causeth them. It helps the plague, sores, boils, itches, the bitings of mad dogs and venomous beasts, all which infirmities are under Mars.' This same writer agrees with Dioscorides that the root of a thistle carried about 'doth expel melancholy and removes all diseases connected therewith.' In other words, the thistle was held to possess all the virtues now claimed for podophyllum, blue-pill, and dandelion—a universal antibilious agent!

But how did the thistle become the emblem of Scotland? Well, there are as many traditions on the subject as there are opinions as to which variety of the plant is the true Scottish thistle. It would be tedious here to refer to all, so let us just note that although the *Carduus Marianus*, or the Blessed or Lady's Thistle—the origin of whose name we have given—is very commonly accepted, so competent an authority on Scottish lore as the author of Nether Lochaber rejects both that and all other varieties in favour of the *Cnicus acaulis*, or the stemless thistle. In doing this, he founds his belief upon the following tradition: Once, during the invasion of Scotland by the Norsemen, the invaders were stealing a march in the dark upon the Scots, when one of the barefooted scouts placed his foot upon a thistle, which caused him to cry out so loudly that the Scots were aroused, and, flying to their horses, drove back the Danes with great slaughter. Now, this could not happen, says Dr. Stewart, with any of the tall thistles, but only with the stemless thistle, which has sharp, fine spikes, and grows close on the ground.

This, at least, is as reasonable an explanation as any of the great national badge of Scotland. It but remains to add that the first mention of the thistle as a national emblem occurs in an inventory of the jewels and other effects of James the Third, about 1467, and its first mention in poetry is in a poem by Dunbar, written about 1503, to commemorate the marriage of James the Fourth with Margaret Tudor, and called The Thrissell and the Rois. The Order of the Thistle dates from James the Seventh of Scotland and Second of England, about 1687.

And now, as we began with the wreath of parsley, which symbolized death, let us end with the crown of orange-blossoms, which, among us, now symbolizes the twofold life of the married state. Among the Greeks, the brides used to wear garlands of myrtle and roses, because both of these plants were associated with the Goddess of Love. In China the orange has, from time immemorial, been an emblem of good luck, and is freely used to present to friends and guests. But although the orange is said to have been first brought by the Portuguese from China in 1547, nevertheless this fruit is supposed to have been the golden apple of Juno, which grew in the Garden of Hesperides. As the golden apple was presented to the Queen of Heaven upon her marriage with Jupiter, we may find here a definite explanation of the meaning attached to the fruit.

But, besides this, it seems that orange-blossom was used centuries ago by Saracen brides in their personal decorations on the great day of their lives. It was meant to typify fruitfulness, and it is to be noted that the orange-tree bears both fruit and blossom at the same time, and is remarkable for its productiveness. It is possible, then, that the idea of orange-blossom for bridal decoration was brought from the East by the Crusaders; but it is uncertain at what date the custom began to be followed in England. However introduced, and whether retained as a symbol or merely for the exquisite beauty of the flower, it will continue to hold its place in the affections of the maiden-bride, to whom it seems to sing:

'Honour, riches, marriage-blessing,
Long continuance and increasing,
Hourly joys be still upon you,
Juno sings her blessings on you.'

CHAPTER X.

ROSEMARY FOR REMEMBRANCE.

'DOTH not Rosemary and Romeo both begin with a letter?' asks Juliet's nurse. Yes, but what did she mean by the query, and by the further remark that 'Juliet hath the prettiest sententions of it, of you and rosemary, that it would do you good to hear it'? For answer we must make some search into the beliefs and customs of the past.

Rosemary is the 'Ros-marinus' of the old herbalists, but it is not a native of Britain, and there is no exact record of when it was introduced here from the South of Europe. Mention of 'Ros-marinus' occurs in an Anglo-Saxon vocabulary of the eleventh century, where it is translated Feld-madder and Sun-dew. There is some doubt whether this has reference to the actual plant now known to us as rosemary, but in no case was it the Rose of Mary, as some have supposed. It is not a rose, and the 'Mary' is from 'marinus,' or 'maris.' The old English spelling was Rosmarin, or Rosmarine; in these forms one finds the word used by Gower, and Shenstone, and other old poets.

In the South of Europe the rosemary has long had magic properties ascribed to it. The Spanish ladies used to wear it as an antidote against the evil eye, and the Portuguese called it the Elfin plant, and dedicated it to the fairies. The idea of the antidote may have been due to a confusion of the name with that of the Virgin; but as a matter of fact the 'Ros-marinus' is frequently mentioned by old Latin writers, including Horace and Ovid. The name came from the fondness of the plant for the sea-shore, where it often gets sprinkled with the 'ros,' or dew of the sea, that is to say, sea-spray. Another cause of confusion, perhaps, was that the leaves of the plant somewhat resemble those of the juniper, which in mediæval times was one of the plants held sacred to the Virgin Mary. In the island of Crete, it is said, a bride dressed for the wedding still calls last of all for a sprig of rosemary to bring her luck.

And thus we come to find rosemary in close association with both marriage and death, just as the hyacinth was, and perhaps still is, among the Greeks. It is interesting to trace the connection by which the same plant came to have two such different uses.

One of the earliest mentions of rosemary in English literature is in a poem of the fourteenth century called 'The Gloriouse Rosemaryne,' which begins thus:

'This herbe is callit rosemaryn,
Of vertu that is gode and fyne;
But all the vertues tell I ne can,
Nor, I trowe, no erthely man.'

Nevertheless, the poet proceeds to record at great length many astounding virtues, including the restoration of youth to the aged by bathing in rosemary water.

The 'cheerful rosemarie' and 'refreshing rosemarine' of Spenser was once a great favourite in England, although now it is hardly allowed garden space. Sir Thomas More said: 'I let it run all over my garden walls, not only because my bees love it, but because 'tis the herb sacred to remembrance, and therefore to friendship: whence a sprig of it hath a dumb language that maketh it the chosen emblem at our funeral wakes and in our burial grounds.'

The popularity of the plant was doubtless due to the long-enduring scent and verdure of the leaves. It is one of the most lasting of evergreens, and the pleasant aromatic odour lingers very long after the leaves have been gathered.

Fragrance and endurance, then, are the characteristics of a plant which came to be commonly accepted as an emblem of constancy, and also of loving remembrance. Thus it is that Herrick sings of it:

'Grow for two ends, it matters not at all,
Be't for my bridal or my burial.'

Thus it is that we find Friar Laurence over Juliet's body, saying:

'Dry up your tears, and stick your rosemary
On this fair corse,'

which is certainly not what the nurse meant when she told Romeo of the 'prettiest sententions.'

High medicinal properties were ascribed to the rosemary, so much so that old Parkinson writes: 'Rosemary is almost as great use as bayes, both for outward and inward remedies, and as well for civill as physicall purposes; inwardly for the head and heart, outwardly for the sinews and joynts; for civill uses, as all do know, at weddings, funerals, etc., to bestow among friends; and the physicall are so many that you might as well be tyred in the reading as I in the writing, if I should set down all that might be said of it.'

One of the 'physicall' uses was in stirring up the tankard of ale or sack, and at weddings a sprig was usually dipped in the loving-cup to give it fragrance as well as luck.

The virtues of the plant are celebrated in a curious wedding sermon quoted by Hone:

'The rosemary is for married men, the which by name, nature, and continued use, man challengeth as properly belonging to himself. It overtoppeth all the flowers in the garden boasting man's rule; it helpeth the brain, strengtheneth the memory, and is very medicinal for the head. Another property is, it affects the heart. Let this ros-marinus, this flower of man, ensign of your wisdom, love, and loyalty, be carried not only in your hands but in your heads and hearts.'

One does not easily reconcile this laudation with the popular superstition that wherever the rosemary flourished there should the woman be the ruling power. And to this superstition, be it noted, has been ascribed the disfavour into which the plant has fallen among gardeners since Shakespeare's time.

The medical properties may have been over-rated by old Parkinson, but some are recognised even to this day. Thus rosemary is used as an infusion to cure headaches, and is believed to be an extensive ingredient in hair-restorers. It is also one of the ingredients in the manufacture of Eau-de-Cologne, and has many other uses in the form of oil of rosemary. It is said that bees which feed on rosemary blossoms produce a very delicately-flavoured honey. Perfumers are greatly indebted to it. According to De Gubernatis, the flowers of the plant are proof against rheumatism, nervous indisposition, general debility, weakness of sight, melancholy, weak circulation, and cramp. Almost as comprehensive a cure as some of our modern universal specifics!

The medicinal properties of rosemary have been held by some to account for its funeral uses. At all events, an ingenious writer of the seventeenth century held that the custom of carrying a sprig at a funeral had its rise from a notion of an 'alexipharmick' or preservative virtue in the herb which would protect the wearer from 'pestilential distempers,' and be a powerful defence 'against the morbid effluvias of the corpse.' For the same reason, this writer asserts, it was customary to burn rosemary in the chambers of the sick, just like frankincense, 'whose odour is not much different from rosemary, which gave the Greeks occasion to call it Libanotis, from Libanos (frankincense).'

The hyssop of the Bible is believed by some to be rosemary, and it is said that in the East it was customary to hang up a bunch in the house as a protection against evil spirits, and to use it in various ceremonies against enchantment. Perhaps there was some connection between this custom and that of the Greeks referred to by Aristotle, who regarded indigestion as the effect of witchcraft, and who used rue as an antidote. The dispelling of the charm was just the natural physical action of the herb.

In Devonshire, however, there was a more mystic use for rosemary in dispelling the charms of witches. A bunch of it had to be taken in the hand and dropped bit by bit on live coals, while the two first verses of the sixty-eighth psalm were recited, followed by the Lord's Prayer. Bay-leaves were sometimes used in the same manner; but if the afflicted one were suffering physically, he had also to take certain prescribed medicines. Rosemary worn about the body was believed to strengthen the memory and to add to the success of the wearer in anything he might undertake.

It is as an emblem of remembrance that rosemary is most frequently used by the old poets. Thus Ophelia:

'There is rosemary for you, that's for remembrance;
I pray you, love, remember.'

And in The Winter's Tale:

'For you there's rosemary and rue; these keep
Seeming and savour all the winter long;
Grace and remembrance be with you both.'

And thus Drayton:

'He from his lass him lavender hath sent,
Showing her love, and doth requital crave;
Him rosemary his sweetheart, whose intent
Is that he her should in remembrance have.'

Quotations might be easily multiplied, but the reader will find in Brand's Popular Antiquities numerous references to the plant by writers of the sixteenth and seventeenth centuries.

As an emblem of rejoicing, rosemary was also often used. Hone quotes a contemporary account of the joyful entry of Queen Elizabeth into London in 1558, wherein occurs this passage: 'How many nosegays did her Grace receive at poor women's hands? How often times stayed she her chariot when she saw any simple body offer to speak to her Grace? A branch of rosemary given to her Grace, with a supplication by a poor woman about Fleet Bridge, was seen in her chariot till her Grace came to Westminster.'

The object of the particular floral offering in this case is not very obvious, unless as an emblematic tribute to the maiden queen.

Rosemary used to be carried in the hand at weddings, as well as strewed on the ground and dipped in the cup. Thus Stow narrates of a wedding in 1560, that 'fine flowers and rosemary were strewed for them coming home'; and Brand cites numerous instances from old plays. In one, 'the parties enter with rosemary, as if from a wedding'; and in Beaumont and Fletcher's Scornful Lady, the question is asked about a wedding, 'Were the rosemary branches dipped?' This dipping, moreover, was in scented water as well as in the loving-cup, and hence the allusion in Dekker's Wonderful Year to a bride who had died on her wedding-night:

'Here is a strange alteration; for the rosemary that was washed in sweet water to set out the bridal is now wet in tears to furnish her burial.'

It is on record that Anne of Cleves wore rosemary at her wedding with Henry the Eighth; and in an account of some marriage festivities at Kenilworth, attended by Queen Elizabeth, there is frequent mention of the plant. An idea of how it was sometimes used is given in a description of a sixteenth century wedding quoted by the Rev. Hilderic Friend: 'The bride being attired in a gown of sheep's russet and a kirtle of fine worsted, attired with abillement of gold' (milliner's French even then!); 'and her hair, yellow as gold, hanging down behind her, which was curiously combed and plaited' she was led to church between two sweet boys, with bride-laces and rosemary tied about her silken sleeves. There was a fair bride-cup of silver-gilt carried before her, wherein was a goodly branch of rosemary gilded very fair, and hung about with silken ribands of all colours.'

Coles says that the garden rosemary was called *Rosmarinus coronarium*, because the women made crowns and garlands of it. Ben Jonson says that it was customary for the bridesmaids to present the bridegroom next morning with a bunch of rosemary. And Brand says that as late as 1698 the custom still prevailed in England of decking the bridal bed with sprigs of rosemary.

In Jonson's Tale of a Tub, one of the characters assembled to await the intended bridegroom says: 'Look an' the wenches ha' not found un out, and do present un with a van of rosemary and bays, enough to vill a bow-pott or trim the head of my best vore-horse; we shall all ha' bride-laces and points, I see.' And again, a country swain assures his sweetheart at their wedding: 'We'll have rosemary and bayes to vill a bow-pott, and with the same I'll trim the vorehead of my best vore-horse'—so that it would seem the decorative use was not confined to the bride, the guests, and the banquet.

As a love-charm the reputation of rosemary seems to have come from the South. There is an old Spanish proverb which runs:

'Who passeth by the rosemarie,
And careth not to take a spray,
For woman's love no care has he,
Nor shall he, though he live for aye.'

Mr. Thiselton-Dyer says that rosemary is used in some parts of the country, as nut-charms are on Halloween, to foretell a lover; only, St. Agnes' Eve is the occasion on which to invoke with a sprig of rosemary, or thyme, with this formula:

'St. Agnes, that's to lovers kind,
Come, ease the troubles of my mind.'

For love-potions, decoctions of rosemary were much employed.

As to funereal uses, those who are familiar with Hogarth's drawings will remember one of a funeral party with sprigs of rosemary in their hands. Misson, a French traveller (*temp.* William the Third), thus describes English funeral ceremonies: 'When they are ready to set out, they nail up the coffin, and a servant presents the company with sprigs of rosemary. Everyone takes a sprig and carries it in his hand till the body is put into the grave, at which time they all throw their sprigs in after it.' Hence Gay:

'To show their love, the neighbours far and near,
Follow'd with wistful looks the damsel's bier;
Sprigg'd rosemary the lads and lasses bore,
While dismally the parson walk'd before.
Upon her grave the rosemary they threw.'

Whether the fact that the rosemary buds in January has anything to do with its funereal uses admits of conjecture, as Sir Thomas Browne would say; but that fact was certainly present to the writer of the following verses, which were worthily rescued by Hone from a 'fugitive copy,' although the writer's name has been lost:

'Sweet-scented flower! who art wont to bloom
On January's front severe,
And o'er the wintry desert drear
To waft thy waste perfume!
Come, thou shalt form my nosegay now,

And I will bind thee round my brow;
And, as I twine the mournful wreath,
I'll weave a melancholy song,
And sweet the strain shall be, and long—
The melody of death.

'Come, funeral flower! who lov'st to dwell
With the pale corse in lonely tomb,
And throw across the desert gloom
A sweet decaying smell.
Come, pressing lips, and lie with me
Beneath the lonely alder-tree,
And we will sleep a pleasant sleep,
And not a care shall dare intrude
To break the marble solitude,
So peaceful and so deep.

'And hark! the wind-god, as he flies,
Moans hollow in the forest trees,
And, sailing on the gusty breeze,
Mysterious music dies.
Sweet flower! the requiem wild is mine.
It warns me to the lonely shrine—
The cold turf-altar of the dead.
My grave shall be in yon lone spot,
Where, as I lie by all forgot,
A dying fragrance thou wilt o'er my ashes shed.'

In South Wales, in Cheshire, and in Bucks, the custom still obtains, according to Mr. Hilderic Friend, for each mourner to carry a sprig of rosemary to the grave, into which it is thrown. For weddings, rosemary was dipped in scented water, but for funerals in plain water. Hence the reference in an old play, quoted by Hone:

'If there be
Any so kind as to accompany
My body to the earth, let them not want
For entertainment. Prythee, see they have
A sprig of rosemary, dipp'd in common water,
To smell at as they walk along the streets.'

In Dekker's Wonderful Year there is a description of a charnel-house pavement strewed with withered rosemary, hyacinth, cypress, and yew. During the Plague rosemary was in such demand for funerals that, says Dekker, what 'had wont to be sold for twelvepence an armfull went now at six shillings a handfull.' Certainly a remarkable rise. What the price was in 1531 we know not; but in an account of the funeral expenses of a Lord Mayor of London, who died in that year, appears an item, 'For yerbes at the bewyral £0 1 0'—which presumably refers to rosemary.

'Cypresse garlands,' wrote Coles, 'are of great account at funeralls among the gentiler sort; but Rosemary and Bayes are used by the commons both at funeralls and weddings. They are all plants which fade not a good while after they are gathered and used, as I conceive, to intimate unto us that the remembrance of the present solemnity might not die presently, but be kept in minde for many yeares.'

We have now seen something of the many significations of rosemary, and find an explanation of why the same plant was used for both weddings and funerals, in the fact that it emblemised remembrance by its evergreen and fragrant qualities. One may have doubts about the truth of the story of the man of whom it is recorded that he wanted to be married again on the day of his wife's funeral because the rosemary which had been used at her burial would come in usefully and economically for the wedding ceremony. But if the story is too good to be true, there is suggestion enough in the circumstance referred to by Shakespeare, that

'Our bridal flowers serve for a buried corpse.'

CHAPTER XI.

HERB OF GRACE.

WHY did Ophelia say: 'There's rue for you, and here's some for me; we may call it herb grace o' Sundays, for you must wear your rue with a difference'? For the same reason that Perdita says, in The Winter's Tale, when welcoming the guests of her reputed father and the shepherd:

'Reverend sirs,
For you there's rosemary and rue; these keep
Seeming and savour all the winter long;
Grace and remembrance be to you both,
And welcome to our shearing.'

Remembrance, as we have already seen in the last chapter, was symbolized by the rosemary, and by both Ophelia and Perdita the rue is taken as the symbol of grace. How this came to be is what we have now to consider; but perhaps Mr. Ellacombe, author of Plant-Lore of Shakespeare, is stretching rather far in suggesting that the rue was implied by Antony, when he used the word 'grace' in addressing the weeping followers (Antony and Cleopatra, Act IV., Scene 2) thus:

'Grace grow where these drops fall.'

What Ophelia said was: 'There's rosemary, that's for remembrance. Pray, love, remember. And there is pansies, that's for thought. There's fennel for you, and columbines. There's rue for you, and here's some for me. We may call it herb-grace o' Sundays. Oh! you may wear your rue with a difference.'

There was a method in her madness, and she was distributing her flowers according to the characters and moods of the recipients. Fennel, for instance, emblemised flattery, and columbine ingratitude. Rue emblemised either remorse or repentance—either sorrow or grace—so 'you may wear your rue with a difference.'

So we find the gardener in Richard II. saying, after the departure of the anxious Queen:

'Here she did fall a tear; here in this place
I'll set a bank of rue, sour herb of grace;
Rue, even for ruth, here shortly shall be seen,
In the remembrance of a weeping Queen.'

The herb was believed to be endowed with high moral and medicinal properties, yet was supposed to prosper better in one's garden if stolen from that of a neighbour. But originally it was associated with sorrow and pity. The word rue is doubtless of the same root as 'ruth,' and to rue is to be sorry for, to have remorse. Ruth is the English equivalent of the Latin *ruta*, and in early English appeared as 'rude.' As regret is always more or less a mark of repentance, it was the most natural thing in the world for the herb of ruth, or sorrow, to become the herb of repentance; and as repentance is a sign of grace, so rue became known as 'herb of grace.' This, in brief, is the connection, but it is worth noting in passing that rue is only once mentioned in the Bible, and then only along with a number of other bitter herbs, and without any special significance.

There is this association between rue and rosemary, that both are natives of some of the more barren coasts of the Mediterranean, and that both were very early admitted to the English herb-garden. The old herbalists make frequent mention of rue, and even in Anglo-Saxon times it seems to have been extensively used in medicine. Three peculiarities—a strong, aromatic smell, a bitter taste, and a blistering quality in the leaves—were quite sufficient to establish it in the pharmacopœia of the herb doctors.

The curative qualities of what Spenser calls the 'ranke-smelling rue' were reputedly of a very varied sort. Most readers will remember the reference in Paradise Lost:

'Michael from Adam's eyes the film removed,
Which the false fruit which promised clearer sight
Had bred; then purged with euphraie and rue
The visual nerve, for he had much to see.'

And perhaps its most popular use was as an eyewash. The old writers have recorded some hidden virtues known only to the animal world, such as that weasels prepared themselves for a rat-fight by a diet of rue. Old Parkinson, the herbalist, says that 'without doubt it is a most wholesome herb, although bitter and strong.' He speaks of a 'bead-rowl' of the virtues of rue, but warns people of the 'too frequent or over-much use thereof.'

As both a stimulant and a narcotic the plant has even now recognised virtues, and is not without its uses in modern medicine. The Italians are said to eat the leaves in salad, but hardly of that species—*Ruta montana*—which botanists say it is dangerous to handle without gloves. Our garden species is *Ruta graveolens* and is used by the French perfumers in the manufacture of 'Thieves Vinegar,' or 'Marseilles Vinegar,' once accounted an effective protection against fevers and all infectious diseases.

A curious instance of the value of the herb in this respect occurred in 1760. In the summer of that year a rumour arose, and rapidly spread in London, that the plague had broken out in St. Thomas's Hospital. Immediately there was what would nowadays be called a 'boom' in rue, the price of which rose forty per cent. in a single day in Covent Garden. To allay the popular alarm a manifesto was issued, signed by the physicians, surgeons, and apothecaries of the hospital, certifying that there were no other than the 'usual' diseases among the patients in the wards.

Another explanation of the origin of the name 'herb of grace' has been given than that referred to above. Warburton, among others, thinks that the name was adopted because the old Romanists used the plant on Sundays in their 'exorcisms.' However this may be, rue, or the herb of grace, has been in this country long accounted an antidote of witchcraft. But then, so it was in the days of Aristotle, before it became 'herb of grace,' and when it was hung round the neck as an amulet. The fact is, however, that rue became an antidote of witchcraft because it had become a noted implement in enchantment.

Through its numerous reputed properties, rue early found its way into the magic cauldron.

'Then sprinkles she the juice of rue,
With nine drops of the midnight dew,
From lunary distilling,'

as Drayton has it. In this incantation, again, we have the association with moonwort; and the connection is further illustrated in an old oracle ascribed to Hecate: 'From a root of wild rue fashion and polish a statue; adorn it with household lizards; grind myrrh, gum, and frankincense with the same reptiles, and let the mixture stand in the air during the waning of a moon; then address your words.'

With regard to the association with moonwort, it is interesting to recall that this is one of the plants supposed to be employed by birds for opening nests and removing impediments. Thus in an anecdote gravely related to Aubrey, we find this virtue mentioned: 'Sir Bennet Hoskins told me that his keeper at his parke at Morehampton, in Herefordshire, did for experiment's sake drive an iron naile thwart the hole of a woodpecker's nest, there being a tradition that the dam will bring some leafe to open it. He layed at the bottom of the tree a cleane sheet, and before many houres passed, the naile came out, and he found a leafe lying by it on the sheete. They say the Moonwort will doe such things.'

On the same subject Coles, the botanist, writes: 'It is said, yea, and believed, that Moonwort will open the locks wherewith dwelling-houses are made fast, if it be put into the keyhole.' And Culpeper, the herbalist, writes thus: 'Moonwort is a herb which, they say, will open locks and unshoe such horses as tread upon it. This some laugh to scorn, and these no small fools neither; but country people that I know call it Unshoe-the-horse. Besides, I have heard commanders say that on White Down in Devonshire, near Tiverton, there were found thirty horseshoes pulled off from the feet of the Earl of Essex's horses, being there drawn up in a body, many of them being newly shod, and no reason known, which caused much admiration.' As well it might! This power of the moonwort is said to be still believed in in Normandy, and a similar virtue was also ascribed to the vervain and the mandrake, both associated with rue.

This curious property of moonwort it is which is referred to in Divine Weekes thus:

'Horses that, feeding on the grassy hills,
Tread upon moonwort with their hollow heels,
Though lately shod, at night go barefoot home,
Their maister musing where their shoes become.
Oh, moonwort! tell me where thou hid'st the smith,
Hammer and pinchers, thou unshodd'st them with?
Alas! what lock or iron engine is't
That can the subtle secret strength resist?
Still the best farrier cannot set a shoe
So sure but thou, so shortly, canst undo.'

The old alchemists, however, had a more profitable use for moonwort than the unshoeing of horses; they employed it for converting quicksilver into pure silver, at a time when that metal was neither 'degraded' nor 'depreciated.'

There is an old and pleasant belief, of which John Ruskin makes effective use in driving home one of his morals, that flowers always bloom best in the gardens of those who love them. One could easily find a rationalistic explanation of this sentiment, of course, but it is akin to a superstition entertained in some parts that wherever the moonwort flourishes the owner of the garden is honest.

The ingredients thrown into the mystic cauldron by European sorcerers were in close imitation of those of the ancient alchemists. Moncure Conway has pointed out that among the ingredients used by English and Scotch witches were plants gathered, as in Egypt, at certain seasons or phases of the moon. Chief among such plants were rue and vervain. The

Druids called vervain the 'Holy herb,' and gathered it when the dog-star rose, placing a sacrifice of honey in the earth from which they removed it.

In old Greece and Rome vervain was sacred to the god of war, and in Scandinavia it was also sacred to Thor. It was, moreover, carried by ambassadors of peace, and was supposed to preserve from lightning any house decorated with it. In later times it was believed that a decoction of vervain and rue, mixed, had such a remarkable effect on gun-metal that anyone using a gun over which the liquid had been poured would shoot 'as straight as a die.' This may be news to our modern musketry instructors.

Had this belief, one may wonder, anything to do with the special effect on the eye always supposed to be possessed by rue? Its virtue as an eye-salve, at any rate, may explain how it came to be regarded as capable of bestowing the 'second sight.' To this day, in the Tyrol it is still believed to confer fine vision. If hallucinations were, as Moncure Conway assumes, the basis of belief in second sight, then we can understand the reputed virtues of rue in its narcotic qualities. We have seen how it came to be called 'herb of grace,' yet some think it got this name through being used in witchcraft by exorcists to try the devil.

Speculating on why herbs and roots should have been esteemed magical, Mr. Andrew Lang concludes that it is enough to remember that herbs really have medicinal properties, and that untutored people invariably confound medicine with magic. Thus it was easy to suppose that a plant possessed virtue not only when swallowed, but when carried in the hand. The same writer examines the theory that rue was the Homeric moly, which in a former chapter we identified with the mandrake. But Lang rejects that theory, and says that rue was called 'herb of grace' and was used for sprinkling holy water because in pre-Christian times it had been supposed to have effect against the powers of evil. The early Christians were thus just endeavouring to combine the old charm of rue with the new potency of holy water.

'Euphrasy and rue,' says Lang, 'were employed to purge and purify mortal eyes. Pliny is very learned about the magical virtues of rue. Just as the stolen potato is sovran for rheumatism, so "rue stolen thriveth the best." The Samoans think that their most valued vegetables were stolen from heaven by a Samoan visitor. It is remarkable that rue, according to Pliny, is killed by the touch of a woman, in the same way as, according to Josephus, the mandrake is tamed. These passages prove that the classical peoples had the same extraordinary superstitions about women as the Bushmen and Red Indians. Indeed, Pliny describes a magical manner of defending the crops from blight by aid of women, which is actually practised in America by the red-man.'

Although rue was found in the witches' cauldron, it is also to be found as a popular specific against the blight of witchcraft. Concerning this, however, Moncure Conway says that 'the only region on the Continent where any superstition concerning rue is found resembling the form it assumed in England as affecting the eye is in the Tyrol, where it is one of five plants—the others being broom-straw, agrimony, maidenhair, and ground-ivy—which are bound together, and believed, if carried about, to enable the bearer to see witches, or if laid over the door, to keep any witch who shall seek to enter fastened on the threshold.'

In Scandinavia and North Germany, St. John's wort was used in much the same way for the same purpose.

As to the vervain, which we have seen to be associated with rue, this is a plant the use of which against witchcraft was more widely distributed, just as its medical virtues were also more extensively known. The vervain, indeed, was a sacred plant among the Greeks, as well as among the Druids, who gathered it with solemn religious ceremonies, as they did the sacred mistletoe. Vervain was most esteemed, however, as a love potion, but the connection between its virtues in this respect, and its power over witches and spirits of evil, opens up a branch of inquiry away from our present purpose.

We speak of vervain in connection with rue, because it was the 'holy herb,' just as rue was the 'herb of grace.' Not only was the vervain sacred among the early Druids, but it acquired an early sanctity among Christians. Thus the legend runs:

'All hail, thou holy herb, vervain,
Growing on the ground;
On the Mount of Calvary
There wast thou found!
Thou helpest many a grief,
And staunchest many a wound;
In the name of sweet Jesu,
I lift thee from the ground.'

Mr. Thiselton-Dyer says that a wreath of vervain is now presented to newly-married brides in Germany, but whether this is a survival of the sanctity of the plant, or of its ancient reputation as a love-philtre and charm, is not very clear.

It is to be feared that vervain has sadly fallen out of favour in this country, although not many years ago a pamphlet was written to recommend the wearing of vervain tied by white satin ribbon round the neck, as preservative against evil influences and infection.

'On the Continent'—rather a wide term—Mr. Hilderic Friend says, 'the three essential plants for composing a magic wreath are rue, crane's-bill, and willow.' The crane's-bill is the Herb Robert, or Robin Hood, and the willow has always been connected with lovers. Such a wreath, then, is made by lovers when they wish to see their 'fate.' Love-sick maidens will employ such a wreath to find out how long they have yet to remain single. They walk backwards towards some selected tree, and as they walk throw the wreath over their heads until it fastens on one of the branches. Failure to 'catch on' requires another backward walk, and so on—each failure to buckle the tree counting as a year of spinsterhood. It seems rather an awkward way of getting at the future, but if not more blind than other processes of love divination, would at least require the guarantee of the absence of tight-lacing among the maidens practising it.

Aristotle mentions the use made by the Greeks of rue as a charm against evil spirits, and he accounts for it, somewhat singularly, by the habit of the Greeks in not sitting down to table with strangers. The explanation is, that when they ate with strangers they were apt to become excited and nervous, and so to eat too rapidly, with the result of flatulence and indigestion. These effects were equivalent to bewitchment, as, indeed, disorders of the digestive organs are frequently regarded by many Eastern peoples even to this day. As rue was found to be an effectual antidote to these distressing symptoms, it became a charm against enchantment.

Among many old-wife recipes for the cure of warts is the use of rue. Most people know the old folk-jingle:

'Ashen tree, ashen tree,
Pray bury these warts of me,'

which has to be accompanied by the thrust of a pin into the bark of the tree. The idea was doubtless to extract the sap, for the application of thistle-juice and the juice of the ranunculus are said to prove efficacious in removing warts. In Devonshire they use the juice of an apple, but in some parts of the country rue is preferred. Other wart-curing plants are the spurge, the poppy, the celandine, the marigold, the briony, and the crowfoot.

As old Michael Drayton remarked:

'In medicine, simples had the power
That none need then the planetary hour
To helpe their workinge, they so juiceful were.'

There is a substratum of truth in this, although it requires a wide stretch of imagination, as well as a profundity of faith, to believe that consumption can be cured by passing the body of the patient three times through a wreath of woodbine cut during the increase of the March moon. Yet to this day some French peasants believe that the curative properties of vervain are most pronounced when the plant is gathered, with proper invocations, at a certain phase of the moon.

The notion that animals are acquainted with the medical properties of plants is an old one, probably older than either Pliny or Aristotle. Our own Gerarde, the herbalist, tells that the name celandine was given to that flower (which Wordsworth loved) from a word meaning swallow, because it is used by swallows to 'restore sight to their young ones when their eyes be put out.'

Then Coles, the old botanist, also writes: 'It is known to such as have skill of Nature what wonderful care she hath of the smallest creatures, giving to them a knowledge of medicine to help themselves, if haply diseases are among them. The swallow cureth her dim eyes with Celandine: the wesell knoweth well the virtue of Herb Grace: the dove the verven: the dogge dischargeth his mawe with a kind of grass: and too long it were to reckon up all the medicines which the beasts are known to use by Nature's direction only.'

A Warwickshire proverb runs to this effect:

'Plant your sage and rue together,
The sage will grow in any weather,'

the meaning of which is not very clear—but obscurity is a common complaint of rhymed proverbs. Another rhyme, however, in which rue appears, has a more practical note:

'What savour is better, if physicke be true,
For places infected, than wormwood and rue?'

Rue, indeed, seems to have been in special request as a disinfectant long before carbolic acid was invented, or Condy heard of, yet, perhaps, containing the germ of the idea materialised in 'Sanitas.' For disinfecting purposes wormwood and rue were used sometimes together, and sometimes separately.

The connection between plants and heraldic badges is often close, and although we do not find rue frequent in heraldry, one curious instance of it is interesting. In 809 an Order was created whereof the collar was made of a design in thistles and rue—the thistle because 'being full of prickles is not to be touched without hurting the skin,' rue because it 'is good against serpents and poison.'

Here we have a suggestion of the lizards of the old oracle quoted above.

CHAPTER XII.

THE ROMANCE OF A VEGETABLE.

THERE used to be a popular acrostic the foundation of which is the subject of much speculation. It turned upon two lines of Scott's famous poem, and ran thus:

'"Charge, Chester, charge!
On, Stanley, on!"
Were the last words of Marmion.
Were I in gallant Stanley's place,
When Marmion urged him to the chase,
A word you then would all espy,
That brings a tear to every eye.'

The answer is 'Onion,' and the speculation which results is: Why does a raw onion make the eyes water?

The Greeks, being aware of this characteristic, called the onion *kromuon*; and when they ate it raw, they prudently closed their eyes.

Shakespeare's players in the Taming of the Shrew knew all about it:

'If the boy have not a woman's gift,
To rain a shower of commanded tears,
An onion will do well for such a shift,
Which in a napkin, being close conveyed,
Shall in despite enforce a watery eye.'

So did Lafeu:

'Mine eyes smell onions, I shall weep anon.'

So also did Domitius Enobarbus, who comforted Antony, on reporting the death of Fulvia, by saying, 'Indeed, the tears live in an onion that should water this sorrow,' and who called himself 'onion-eyed' when the Roman addressed his followers before the battle.

The fact, then, has been known for centuries, but the explanation only since chemistry came to be applied to matters of common life. The onion belongs to the genus *Allium*, all the species of which possess a peculiar, pungent, acrid juice, with a powerful odour. The garlic has a stronger smell than the onion, but the onion has more of the volatile oil which all the members of the genus possess.

The constituents which make the genus valuable as food are: albumen, sugar, mucilage, phosphate of lime, and certain salts. All the members of the onion tribe yield a heavy volatile oil when distilled with water—an oil so pungent and concentrated that an ounce of it will represent the essence of forty pounds of garlic. This oil is a compound of sulphur, carbon, and hydrogen, and is called sulphide of allyl, because of its origin in the allium tribe. It is the more volatile, sulphurous fumes of this oil which ascend as an onion is cut that cause the eyes to water, just as sulphur fumes do anywhere. It is the less volatile portion of the oil which gives such permanence and adhesiveness to the onion odour as to render a knife that has been used to cut one offensive for a long time afterwards, in spite of washing.

In the Arabian Nights the purveyor for the Sultan of Casgar tells a story of a man who lost his thumbs and great-toes through eating garlic. This was a youth who had married a beauteous bride, but was unfortunate enough on his marriage-day to eat of a dish strongly flavoured with garlic. The lady was so annoyed that she ordered the bridegroom to be bound, and his thumbs and toes cut off, as punishment for presuming to come to her without first purifying his fingers. Ever afterwards the unfortunate husband always washed his hands one hundred and twenty times with alkali, after dining off a garlic ragout, for, of course, he did not use a fork. But had he known Menander the Greek's receipt, he might have saved his digits. This was to roast beetroot on hot embers for the removal of the odour of garlic.

It might be more generally known that if either walnuts, or raw parsley, be eaten along with onions, the smell of the latter will be destroyed, and digestion of them assisted.

There is, one must admit, a certain association of vulgarity with the onion. It is a valuable food, and an indispensable accessory to the culinary artist; but as used by many people it is not suggestive of refinement. And yet the bulb has not only an honourable character—it has a sort of sacred history.

Both Pliny and Juvenal, among old writers, and many Egyptologists of our own time and country, have recorded that the ancient Egyptians worshipped the onion. It is true that Wilkinson, who wrote on the Manners and Customs of the Ancient Egyptians, doubts the evidence of this; but he adds that the onion was admitted as a common offering on every altar, and that the priests were forbidden to eat it. In Ellis's History of Madagascar it is noted that the Malagasy of our time regard the onion as unclean, and forbidden by the idols. The symbolization of the universe in the concentric folds of the onion may be taken as an explanation of the high reverence in which it was assuredly held by some ancient races.

Whether or not the onion was sacred in Egypt, the garlic, as Herodotus tells us, was the daily food of the Egyptian labourer. And the Jews, when they left Egypt, looked back with fondness to these delicacies. 'We remember the fish which we did eat freely in Egypt, the cucumbers, and the melons, and the leeks, and the onions, and the garlic,' so they told Moses. The onion is still a common food in Egypt, and sometimes almost the only one of the poorer classes. Moreover, the onions of Egypt are much sweeter than, and superior in quality to, those of Europe. It is also noteworthy that the onion grows coarser and more bitter as it is traced northward.

Herodotus says that sixteen hundred talents were expended on garlic, onions, and radishes for the workmen during the building of the Pyramids; and it is recorded that an onion taken from the sarcophagus of an Egyptian mummy two thousand years old was planted and made to grow. We have also the authority of Pliny for what he calls the foolish superstition of the Egyptians in swearing by garlic and onions, calling these vegetables to witness when taking an oath.

Botanists seem now agreed that the original habitat of the onion was the mountainous region of Central Asia; and, according to the *Gardener's Chronicle*, it is still found in a wild state in the Himalayas.

The Mohammedans do not seem to have reverenced the *Allium* tribe. On the contrary, they have a tradition that when Satan stepped out of the Garden of Eden after the fall of man, garlic sprang up where he planted his left foot, and onion where he planted his right foot. This is the reason alleged why Mohammed could never bear the smell of either, and even fainted when he saw them.

Among the Greeks both onions and garlic were held in high regard, both as articles of food and as medicaments. Theophrastus wrote a book on onions, as did also Palladius. Then Homer tells that the onion was an important part of the banquet that Hecamede spread before Nestor and Machaon:

'Before them first a table fair she spread,
Well polished, and with feet of solid bronze;
On this a brazen canister she placed,
And Onions as a relish to the wine,
And pale, clear honey, and pure barley meal.'

Among the Romans the onion seems to have been the common food of the people, although Horace could not understand how they digested it. Its use for promoting artificial tears was also well understood by them, for Columella speaks of *Lacrymosa cæpe,* and Pliny of *Cæpis odor lacrymosus.* Ovid, again, says that both onions and sulphur were given to criminals to purify them from their crimes, upon the old theory of purgation by fumigation. The Romans thought not only that the onion gave strength to the human frame, but that it would also improve the pugnacious quality of their gamecocks. Horace, however, thought that garlic was a fit poison for anybody who committed parricide. The Emperor Nero, on the other hand, thought that eating leeks improved the human voice, and as he was ambitious of being a fine singer, he used to have a leek diet on several days in each month.

The onion tribe must have been held in reverence elsewhere than in Egypt, for, according to Mr. Thiselton-Dyer, in Poland the flower-stalk of the leek is placed in the hands of Christ in pictures and statues.

On Halloween, in some parts of the country, girls attempt a method of divination by means of a 'Saint Thomas onion.' They peel it, wrap it up in a clean handkerchief, and, placing it under their heads, repeat the following rhyme:

'Good St. Thomas, do me right,
And see my true love come to-night,
That I may see him in the face,
And him in my kind arms embrace.'

On the other hand, to dream of an onion is supposed in some parts to foretell sickness.

Or else:

'To dream of eating onions means
Much strife in the domestic scenes,
Secrets found out, or else betrayed,
And many falsehoods made and said.'

It is also a portent of the weather:

'Onion's skin very thin,
Mild winter's coming in;
Onion's skin thick and tough,
Coming winter cold and rough.'

It was the practice in some places to hang up or burn an onion as a safeguard against witchcraft, and the theory of this was that the devil respected it because it was an ancient object of worship. This seems a survival of the Egyptian story; but Mr. Hilderic Friend says that the Arabs, Chinese, and many other peoples, to this day employ onions, leeks, or garlic for preventing witchcraft, and that he himself has frequently seen them tied up with a branch of sago-palm over the doors of Eastern houses for this purpose.

The old custom of throwing an onion after a bride is doubtless well known. It had the same origin as the old Scotch custom of throwing a besom after a cow on its way to market, to avert the evil-eye, and insure luck.

The idea of bad dreams being associated with the onion seems due to the old herbalists. At all events, Coghan wrote in 1596: 'Being eaten raw, they engender all humourous and contemptible putrefactions in the stomacke, and cause fearful dreams, and, if they be much used, they snarre the memory and trouble the understanding.'

Old Gerarde had no opinion of the medical properties of the tribe. Of both leeks and garlic he wrote most disparagingly, as 'yielding to the body no nourishment at all,' but 'ingendereth naughty and sharpe bloud.'

Some of the other old herbalists treat it more kindly, and some ascribe almost every virtue to garlic and onion. Garlic came to be known as 'Poor Man's Treacle,' and in some old works is thus often described. But the word treacle here has no reference to molasses, and is probably derived from the Greek *theriakos*, meaning venomous, for garlic was regarded as an antidote against poison, and as a remedy for the plague.

Pliny long ago wrote of garlic as a remedy for many of the mental and physical ailments of the country people. It was used by the Romans to drive away snakes; and the Romans seem to have adopted this idea from the ancient Greeks. It was recommended by one old English writer as a capital thing with which to frighten away birds from fruit-trees; and has been recently recommended, in solution, as the best preservative of picture-frames from the defilement of flies. Bacon gravely tells of a man who lived for several days on the smell of onions and garlic alone; and there was an old belief that the garlic could extract all the power from a loadstone.

The belief that the eating of onions will acclimatize a traveller seems not uncommon in Eastern countries. Thus, in Burnes' Travels into Bokhara it is recorded that at Peshawur 'Moollah Nujieb suggested that we should eat onions in all the countries we visited, as it is a popular belief that a foreigner becomes acclimated from the use of that vegetable.'

And in Morier's Travels in Persia it is said: 'Those who seek for sulphur, which is found at the highest accessible point of the mountain of Damarvend, go through a course of training previous to the undertaking, and fortify themselves by eating much of garlic and onions.'

The general explanation given of how the leek became the emblem of Wales, and is worn on St. David's Day, is this: In 640 King Cadwallader gained a complete victory over the Saxons, owing to the special interposition of St. David, who ordered the Britons always to wear leeks in their caps, so that they might easily recognise each other. As the Saxons had no such recognisable headmark, they attacked each other as foes, and aided in their own defeat.

There is a more poetic story. It is that St. David lived in the valley of Ewias, in Monmouthshire, spending his time in contemplation:

'And did so truly fast
As he did only drink what crystal Hodney yields,
And fed upon the leeks he gathered in the fields,
In memory of whom, in each revolving year,
The Welshmen, on his day, that sacred herb do wear.'

St. David, however, died in 544, and therefore it is probable that the leek was a common and favourite vegetable in Wales during his lifetime—that is to say, more than thirteen hundred years ago. A still more prosaic explanation of the Welsh emblem is sometimes offered. It is that it originated in a custom of the Welsh farmers when helping each other in a neighbourly way to take their leeks and other vegetable provender with them. Now, as the word leek is from the Anglo-Saxon *leac*, which originally meant any vegetable, it is probable enough that the Saxons sneeringly applied the word to the Welsh on account of their vegetarian proclivities. We cannot, of course, be sure that the leek was worn as a badge in Cadwallader's time, but we have at any rate Shakespeare's authority for concluding that it was worn by the Welsh soldiers at the Battle of Poitiers in 1356.

The phrase 'to eat the leek'—meaning to retract and 'knuckle-under'—is supposed to have originated in that famous scene in Shakespeare's Henry the Fifth, where Fluellan the Welshman compels Pistol to swallow the vegetable at which he had been expressing such abhorrence. But there is earlier evidence that the leek was regarded as something ignominious in England. Thus in Chaucer:

'The beste song that ever was made
Is not worth a leke's blade,
But men will tend ther tille.'

Without dwelling on the culinary uses of the onion tribe, which have been exhaustively described by others, a few applications, not generally known, may be briefly noted.

In olden times there was a famous ointment called Devil's Mustard, which was supposed to cure cancer, remove tumours, and so forth. It was a compound of garlic and olive-oil, and had a smell which was enough to frighten away any disease—or else to create one. Then the fair dames of old had a favourite cosmetic for the hands and face, and one also which was used as an antiseptic, which was largely composed of garlic. Leek ointment, again, made of pounded leeks and hog's lard, was used as a liniment for burns and scalds.

It is said that in India, where dyspepsia is common, garlic is found to be a great palliative. It is in many countries regarded as a sure antidote against contagion; and persons have been known to put a small piece in the mouth before approaching the bed of a fever-stricken patient. Whether it has any real virtue of the kind one may doubt, but let us hope that it has more than is ascribed to some so-called disinfectants—the power to kill one bad smell with another.

In The Family Dictionary, popular in our grandfathers' time, appears the following certain remedy for the plague: 'Take away the core of an onion, fill the cavity with treacle dissolved or mixed with lemon-juice, stop up the hole with the slice you have cut off, roast the whole on hot ashes so long till well incorporated and mixed together, then squeeze out the juice of the roasted onion, and give it to a person seized with the plague. Let him presently lie down in his bed and be well covered up that he may perspire. This is a remedy that has not its equal for the plague, provided the patient perspires presently.'

And if it did promote perspiration, one can well believe that it might be curative.

Not only has garlic been esteemed as an antidote to the bite of snakes, but it has also been regarded as a cure for hydrophobia, while onions have been claimed as a cure for small-pox, and leeks as an antidote for poisonous fungi. Old Celsus, from whom Paracelsus took his name, regarded several of the onion tribe as valuable in cases of ague, and Pliny had the same belief. In our own time the onion is held to be an excellent anti-scorbutic, and is thought to be more useful on ship-board than lime-juice in preventing scurvy.

In fact, in all skin diseases, and in many inflammatory disorders, preparations of the onion have a real value. The juice is also useful in stopping bleeding, although one may hesitate to believe, as was popularly supposed, that a drop of it will cure earache, and that persistent application will remove deafness.

There still exists, however, a belief that onion-juice is the best hair-restorer in the market, in spite of its disagreeable smell.

It would take too long to mention all the virtues that have been claimed, with more or less reason, for all the members of the *Allium* genus, but it is a curious fact that the onion, which relieves dyspepsia and aids the digestion of some, is a certain cause of indigestion in others. Is it not said that Napoleon, who was a martyr to indigestion, lost the Battle of Leipsic through having partaken of a too hurried meal of beefsteak and onions? It is a savoury dish, but has worked woe to many. One does not wonder that the old writers declared that onions brought bad dreams—if they were eaten raw, or badly cooked, at late supper.

It is open to grave doubt whether the author of The Family Dictionary was right in saying that 'they that will eat onions daily will enjoy better health than otherwise.' What is one man's meat is another man's poison; and certainly there is no article in common use which produces such opposite effects upon the human system as the onion. It has often been found beneficial to individuals in feverish attacks, and yet the malingerers in our garrison hospitals know well how to promote febrile symptoms by a hearty consumption of garlic.

A fitting conclusion to this chapter will be the summary of Sir John Sinclair, the author of a Code of Health and Longevity:

'Onyons in physick winneth no consent,
To cholerick folke they are no nutriment;
By Galen's rule, such as phlegmatic are
A stomacke good within them do prepare.
Weak appetites they comfort, and the face
With cheerful colour evermore they grace,
And when the head is naked left of hair,
Onyons, being sod or stamp'd, again repair.'

CHAPTER XIII.

THE STORY OF A TUBER.

THE planting of a tuber by Clusius, in 1588, in the Botanical Gardens at Vienna, is often referred to as the introduction of the potato into Europe. As a matter of fact, however, this was not the first planting, for the Spaniards brought the real potato—*Solanum tuberosum*—home to Spain about 1580. From Spain it extended to Italy, and became at once a common article of food there. From Spain it also extended to Belgium, and was cultivated there; and it was from a Belgian that Clusius got the roots which he planted at Vienna in 1588.

Then, again, it has been said that Christopher Columbus was the first European who ever tasted a potato, and that was in 1492, when he reached Cuba. From Cuba he brought samples back with him to Genoa. This would make our history one hundred years older, only it so happens that the *Solanum tuberosum* is not a native of these parts, and could not have been at Cuba when Columbus was there. What he tasted and brought home was the *Convolvulus batatas*, or sweet potato, a very different article, although it gave its name, 'batatas,' to our tuber in the modified form of 'potato.'

The real potato is a native of Chili, and it has been proved to the satisfaction of naturalists that it did not exist in North America before the arrival of Europeans. How, then, could Sir John Hawkins bring it from Santa-Fé in 1565, or Sir Walter Raleigh from Virginia in 1584? Well, in the first place, it was the sweet potato that Sir John brought; and in the second place, before Sir Walter went to Virginia, the Spaniards had brought there the real potato on returning from some of their South American expeditions. In 1580 they sent it home, and there is evidence that by 1580 the *Solanum tuberosum* had been planted in North America. By the time Raleigh brought it to England, however, it was already a familiar root in Italy.

But did he bring it? There are some who say that it was Sir Francis Drake who brought the roots and presented them to Sir Walter Raleigh, who planted them on his estate near Cork in the year 1594. M'Culloch, however, says that 1610 was the year of the introduction into Ireland, and other writers say that Raleigh knew so little of the virtues of the plant he was naturalizing that he caused the apples, not the tubers, to be cooked and served upon his own table. Buckle, however, says that the common, or Virginian, potato was introduced by Raleigh in 1586, and Lyte, who wrote in that year, does not mention the plant; but Gerarde, who published the first edition of his Herbal in 1597, gave a portrait of himself with a potato in his hand.

Here, then, we have some negative certainties and some positive uncertainties. Columbus did not take the real potato to Genoa in 1492; Hawkins did not bring it to England in 1565. The Spaniards did take it to Spain in or about 1580; but whether Raleigh was the first to bring it to Britain, and in what year, remains open to doubt.

During the whole of the seventeenth century the potato was quite a rarity in this country, and up to 1684 was cultivated only in the gardens of the gentry. In Scotland it does not seem to have been grown at all, even in gardens, before 1728. Phillips, in the History of Cultivated Vegetables, says that in 1619 the price in England was one shilling a pound. He further says that great prejudices existed against it, that it was alleged to be poisonous, and that in Burgundy the cultivation of it was prohibited.

These early prejudices against the potato are explainable on the supposition that the people did not know how to cook it, and possibly ate it raw, in which state it is certainly unwholesome, if not actually poisonous. Then, again, it belongs to a family of ill-repute, the *Solanacæ*, of which the deadly nightshade and the mandrake are members, as well as more honoured specimens like the tomato, tobacco, datura, and cayenne-pepper plants. The mandrake, of course, was the subject of ancient dislike, and perhaps it was natural for our superstitious progenitors to regard with suspicion any relative of that lugubrious root.

Even the tempting appearance of the tomato did not suffice to win favour for it when first introduced into Europe, until somebody discovered that, although undoubtedly sent by the infidels to poison the Christians, the Bon Dieu had interfered, and transformed it into an agreeable and wholesome fruit.

One meets with two references to the potato in Shakespeare, and these are said to be the earliest notices of it in English literature. Thus in Troilus and Cressida: 'The devil luxury, with his fat rump, and potato finger, tickles these together!' In the Merry Wives, Falstaff says: 'Let the sky rain potatoes; let it thunder to the time of Green Sleeves; hail kissing-comfits, and snow Eringoes.'

There are several references in the early dramatists, which the curious reader may find collected in a note in Steevens's Shakespeare, but which hardly serve our purpose. There is one reference, however, by Waller, which is interesting:

'With candy'd plantains and the juicy pine,
On choicest melons and sweet grapes they dine,
And with potatoes fat their wanton kine,'

because it seems to be the case that, prior to 1588, the Italian peasants used the potato as food for their pigs as well as for themselves.

We are constrained, however, to conclude that Shakespeare and the old dramatists referred to the sweet potato, sometimes called the Spanish potato. 'Eringoes,' mentioned by Falstaff, were candied roots. Eringo is curiously suggestive of 'Gringo,' which was the name of contempt applied by the Spaniards to all foreigners, but especially Englishmen. The word would seem to have been imported by the gentlemen-adventurers from the Spanish Main, in the time of Good Queen Bess. If we take 'candied roots' in association with 'kissing-comfits,' we are compelled to conclude that Falstaff's potato was the 'batatas,' the sweet, fleshy roots of which were described by Columbus to be 'not unlike chestnuts in taste.'

Certain it is that the potato was not regarded in this country as an object of national importance until 1662, when the Royal Society advised that it should be planted. In the history of the Society there is the record of a recommendation of a committee, dated 1662, urging all the Fellows who possessed land to plant potatoes, and persuade their friends to do the same, 'in order to alleviate the distress that would accompany a scarcity of food.'

In Scotland, the first mention of the potato occurs in the household book of the Duchess of Buccleuch and Monmouth. From Chambers's Traditions of Edinburgh we learn that the price in 1701 was half-a-crown a peck. Robertson, of Irvine discovered what he thought the earliest evidence of potatoes in Scotland in the household book of the Eglinton family. The date of this entry, however, was 1733, and Robert Chambers showed that the date in the Buccleuch book was thirty-two years earlier.

Further information is given by the Duke of Argyle in Scotland As It Was, And As It Is. There we learn that, until long past the middle of the eighteenth century, little or nothing was known of the potato in Scotland, although in after years it brought about the most prodigious effects on the population. The Celts of Ireland first began to use it as an adjunct, and then as a main article of food. From them it passed over to the Celts of the Hebrides, and was introduced into South Uist by Macdonald of Clanranald in 1743. The Highlanders, always suspicious of novelties, resisted the use of it for some years; and the neighbouring island of Bernera was not reached until 1752. It was soon found, however, that the tuber would grow luxuriantly almost anywhere—even on sand, and shingle, and in bogs. It was quickly planted in those patches of ditched-off land known in the

Highlands as 'lazy beds'—a not inappropriate term, which in Ireland is applied to patches of potatoes not sown in drills.

In Ireland and in the Highlands it quickly came to be the main food of the people during the greater portion of the year; but in the Lowlands of Scotland, and the rural districts of England, it was only used as a food accessory, though it soon became an important article of commerce. It has often happened that the potato crops have realized higher prices than any other product of the farm.

It has been sometimes stated that the man who planted the first field of potatoes in Scotland died within the last forty years. This is an error. The first field planted in the Lowlands was at Liberton Muir, about the year 1738, by a farmer named Mutter, who died in 1808. An attempt had been made some years earlier by a farm-labourer, named Prentice, near Kilsyth, but not as a farming operation.

In any case we do not get farther back than about 1730 for potato-planting in Scotland, whereas in England, by 1684 the recommendations of the Royal Society had been largely adopted, especially in Lancashire, where the first serious beginning seems to have been made. On the other hand, the cultivation has not extended so rapidly in England as in either Ireland or Scotland.

The annual crop of Ireland is estimated as, on the average, equal to about one thousand three hundred and twenty pounds per inhabitant; that of Scotland, about three hundred and ninety pounds; and that of England, about one hundred and twenty pounds. Germany is the next largest producer to Ireland, and also the next largest consumer—the crops being equal to about one thousand and sixty pounds per head. Holland and Belgium each produce about five hundred and eighty pounds, and France about five hundred and fifty pounds, of potatoes per inhabitant per annum.

It is curious that, although Spain and Italy were the first cultivators and users in Europe, the product of each of these countries is now only about fifty-five pounds per head.

The annual value of the entire potato crop of Europe may be stated at about one hundred and sixty million pounds; and that of the United Kingdom at about one-tenth of this total. That of North America is about twenty million pounds more; and it is a curious instance of the vagaries of time that the *Solanum tuberosum* is now known in America as the 'Irish potato,' to distinguish it from the batatas, or sweet potato.

All this immense development of cultivation does not complete the topographical record of our tuber. It has been introduced into India, and is now successfully cultivated both in Bengal and in the Madras Presidency. It has found a home in the Dutch East Indies and in China; and its tastes and habits are affectionately studied in Australia. But as in the tropics it has to be grown at an altitude of three thousand feet, or more, above sea-level, it can never become so common in hot countries as in Europe.

It is not only as a food-plant that the potato has secured the respect and affection of mankind. Starch is made from it both for the laundry and for the manufacture of farina, dextrin, etc. The dried pulp from which the starch has been extracted is used for making boxes. From the stem and leaves an extract is made of a narcotic, used to allay pain in coughs and other ailments. In a raw state the potato is used as a cooling application for burns and sores. A spirit is distilled from the tuber, which in Norway is called 'brandy,' and in other places is used for mixing with malt and vine liquors. Many of the farinaceous preparations now so popular in the nursery and sick-room are made largely of potato-starch; and in some places cakes and puddings are made from potato-flour.

To the potato are also ascribed properties of another kind. The folklore of the plant is meagre, considering its wide distribution, but there are a number of curious superstitions connected with it. In some parts there is a belief that it thrives best if planted on Maundy Thursday; in others, that if planted under certain stars it will become watery. In Devonshire the people believe that the potato is a certain cure for the toothache—not taken internally, but carried about in the pocket. It is by several writers mentioned as a reputed cure for rheumatism in the same way; only it is prescribed that, in order to be an effective cure in such cases, the potato should be stolen. Mr. Andrew Lang mentions an instance of faith in the practice of this cure, which he came across in a London drawing-room. He regards this belief as a survival of the old superstitions about mandrake, and as analogous to the habit of African tribes who wear roots round the neck as protection against wild animals.

The value of the potato as food has been much discussed; but it seems to rank next to the plantain, and a long way behind either rice or wheat. The author of the Chemistry of Common Life has pointed to the remarkable physiological likeness of tribes of people who live chiefly on rice, plantain, and potato. The Hindu, the negro, and the Irishman are all remarkable for being round-bellied, and this peculiarity is ascribed to the necessity of consuming a large bulk of food in order to obtain the requisite nourishment.

It is not, of course, the root of the plant which we consume. The tubers known to the table are the swollen portions of the underground branches, and the so-called 'eyes' are really leaf-buds. It is by cuttings from these tubers, however, that the plant is mostly propagated. About three-fourths of the weight of the potato is water, and this may explain the injurious effect which excessive rainfall has on the crops. The disease which attacks the plant, and has been the cause of Irish famines, past and prospective, is a species of fungus, which first attacks and discolours the straws, and then spreads downwards to the tubers, increasing the quantity of water in them, reducing the quantity of starch, and converting the albumen into casein.

When this disease once appears it is apt to spread over wide areas where the same climatic influences prevail, and when the disease appears in any strength the crops are rapidly rendered unfit for human food. The trouble of the Irish peasantry of the West is that they have no alternative crop to fall back on when the potato fails. Their plots are too small for cereals, and they cannot be persuaded to cultivate cabbages and other vegetables along with their tubers. It is thus that, when the day of tribulation comes, the potato appears to be really a curse rather than a blessing to agricultural Ireland.

There have been frequent projects for reverting to original types—that is to say, for obtaining a fresh supply of the indigenous plant from South America, and breeding a new stock, as it were. It is a possible mode of extirpating the disease which may be resorted to.

The Irish famine of 1847 was due to the failure of the potato crops in 1846, preceded by two or three years of bad crops. This failure was due to disease, and the eating of the diseased tuber brought on a pestilence, so that altogether the deaths by starvation and epidemics in that disastrous period amounted to nearly a million and a quarter persons. To deal with the distress various sums were voted by Parliament to the total amount of over ten millions sterling. This was supplemented by private philanthropy in this country, and by generous aid from the United States and some European countries. What was the actual money cost to the world at large of the failure of the Irish potato crop in 1846 can never be accurately known; but the amount was so enormous as to create a serious economic problem in connection with the homely tuber.

There have been several partial failures since in Ireland, although nothing so extensive as that of 1846, and in 1872 the disease was very bad in England. In that year, indeed, the importation of foreign potatoes rose to the enormous value of one million six hundred and fifty-four thousand pounds to supply our own deficient crops. In 1876, again, there was great excitement and alarm about the 'Colorado beetle,' an importation from America, which was destined, it was said, to destroy all our potato-fields. But the beetle proved comparatively harmless, and seems now to have disappeared from these shores.

The Englishman and Scotchman cannot do without his potato as an adjunct; but the error of the Irishman is in making it the mainstay of his life. The words of Malthus in this connection put the matter in a nutshell, much as he has been abused for his theory of the effects of the potato on population. 'When the common people of a country,' he says, 'live principally upon the dearest grain, as they do in England on wheat, they have great resources in a scarcity, and barley, oats, rice, cheap soups, and potatoes, all present themselves as less expensive, yet, at the same time, wholesome means of nourishment; but when their habitual food is the lowest in this scale, they appear to be absolutely without resource, except in the bark of trees—like the poor Swedes—and a great portion of them must necessarily be starved.'

CHAPTER XIV.

THE CENTRE OF THE WORLD.

WHERE is it? 'At Charing Cross, of course,' says the self-assured Londoner; and in one sense he may not be far wrong. 'At Boston,' says the cultured inhabitant of the 'hub' of the universe. 'Wherever I am,' says the autocrat who essays to sway the destinies of nations. Well, we all know the story of the Head of the Table, and even if we did not know it, instinct would tell us where to look. But the centre of the world, in an actual, physical, racial, and mundanely comprehensive sense—where is it?

One does not find it so easy to answer the question as did good old Herodotus, who scouted as absurd the idea of the earth being circular. 'For my own part,' says the Father of History—and of lies, according to some people—'I cannot but think it exceedingly ridiculous to hear some men talk of the circumference of the Earth, pretending without the smallest reason or probability that the ocean encompasses the Earth, that the Earth is round as if mechanically formed so, and that Asia is equal to Europe.'

Herodotus found no difficulty in describing the figure and size of the portions of the earth whose existence he recognised, but then he said, 'from India eastward the whole Earth is one vast desert, unknown and unexplored.' And for long after Herodotus, the Mediterranean was regarded as the central sea of the world, and in the time of Herodotus, Rhodes was accounted the centre of that centre.

It is very interesting, however, to trace how many centres the world has had in its time—or rather within the range of written history. The old Egyptians placed it at Thebes, the Assyrians at Babylon, the Hindus at Mount Meru, the Jews at Jerusalem, and the Greeks at Olympus, until they moved it to Rhodes. There exists an old map in which the world is represented as a human figure, and the heart of that figure is Egypt. And there exists, or did exist, an old fountain in Sicily on which was this inscription: 'I am in the centre of the garden; this garden is the centre of Sicily, and Sicily is the Centre of the whole Earth.'

It is a grand thing to be positive in assertion when you are sure of your ground, and the builder of this fountain seems to have been sure of his. But then other people can be positive too, and in that vast desert eastward of India, imagined by Herodotus, there is the country of China, which calls itself the Middle Kingdom, and the Emperor of which, in a letter to the

King of England in this very nineteenth century, announced that China is endowed by Heaven as the 'flourishing and central Empire' of the world.

And yet, once upon a time, according to some old Japanese writings, Japan was known as the Middle Kingdom; and the Persians claimed the same position for Persia; and according to Professor Sayce, the old Chaldeans said that the centre of the earth was in the heart of the impenetrable forest of Eridu.

This forest, by the way, was also called the 'holy house of the Gods,' but it does not seem to have had anything to do with the Terrestrial Paradise, the exact location of which Mr. Baring-Gould has laboriously tried to identify through the legends of the nations. It is a curious fact that a ninth-century map, in the Strasburg Library, places the Terrestrial Paradise—the Garden of Eden—in that part of Asia we now know as the Chinese Empire, and it is also so marked in a map in the British Museum.

In a letter supposed to have emanated from the mysterious if not mythical Prester John, it is written: 'The river Indus which issues out of Paradise flows among the plains through a certain province, and it expands, embracing the whole province with its various windings. There are found emeralds, sapphires, carbuncles, topazes, chrysolites, onyx, beryl, sardius, and many other precious stones. There, too, grows the plant called Asbestos.'

And all this was reported to be just three days' journey from the garden from which Adam was expelled, but as the geographical position of the province was not specified the information was a trifle vague. Prester John, however, described a wonderful fountain, the virtues of which correspond with those of a well in Ceylon described by Sir John Mandeville, and this is why some people say that the Garden of Eden was in the Island of Spices.

There is a twelfth-century map of the world at Cambridge, which shows Paradise on an island opposite the mouth of the Ganges. And in the story of St. Brandan, the saint reaches an island somewhere 'due east from Ireland,' which was Paradise, and on which he met with a man who told him that a stream—which no living being might cross—flowing through the island, divided the world in twain. Another centre!

In an Icelandic story of the fourteenth century are related the marvellous adventures of one Eirek of Drontheim, who, determined to find out the Deathless Land, made his way to Constantinople. There he received a lesson in geography from the Emperor. The world, he was told, was precisely one hundred and eighty thousand stages, or about one million English miles, round, and is not propped up on posts, but is supported by the will of God. The distance between the earth and heaven, he was told, is one hundred thousand and forty-five miles, and round about the earth is a big sea called the ocean.

'But what is to the south of the earth?' asked the inquisitive Eirek.

'Oh,' replied the Emperor, 'the end of the earth is there, and it is called India.'

'And where shall I find the Deathless Land?' he inquired; and he was told that slightly to the east of India lies Paradise.

Thereupon Eirek and a companion started across Syria, took ship and arrived at India, through which they journeyed on horseback till they came to a strait which separated them from a beautiful land. Eirek crossed over and found himself in Paradise, and, strange to say, an excellent cold luncheon waiting for him. It took him seven years to get home again, and, as he died soon after his return, the map of the route was lost.

Still, Eirek's Paradise may not improbably have been Ceylon.

The latest location of the Garden of Eden is by a recent traveller in Somaliland, in the north-east shoulder of Africa and south of the Gulf of Aden. This is in the neighbourhood of the country of Prester John, but in its present aspects can by no means be regarded as a Terrestrial Paradise.

Sir John Mandeville's description of the Terrestrial Paradise which he discovered gives it as the highest place on the earth—so high that the waters of the Flood could not reach it. And in the very centre of the highest point is a well, he said, that casts out the four streams, Ganges, Nile, Tigris, and Euphrates—all sacred streams. Now, in the Encyclopædia of India it is stated that 'The Hindus at Bikanir Rajputana taught that the mountain Meru is in the centre surrounded by concentric circles of land and sea. Some Hindus regard Mount Meru as the North Pole. The astronomical views of the Puranas make the heavenly bodies turn round it.' So here again we have a mountain as the terrestrial centre.

In the Avesta there is reference to a lofty mountain at the centre of the world from which all the mountains of the earth have grown, and at the summit of which is the fountain of waters, whereby grow two trees—the Heavenly Soma, and another tree which yields all the seeds that germinate on earth. From this fountain, according to the Buddhist tradition, flow four streams to the four points of the compass, each of them making a complete circuit in its descent.

This central mountain is the Navel of Waters where originated all matter, and where sits Yama under the Soma tree—just as in the Norse legend the Norns, or Fates, sit by the great central earth-tree, Yggdrasil.

According to the Greek tradition, Jupiter, in order to settle the true centre of the earth, sent out two eagles, one from east and one from west. They met on the spot on which was erected the Temple of Delphi, and a stone in the centre of that temple was called the Navel of the World. A golden eagle was placed on each side of this stone. The design is preserved in many examples of Greek sculpture, and the stone itself is mentioned in several of the Greek plays.

With reference to this, Mr. Lethaby, in his Architecture, Mysticism, and Myth, observes: 'We may see embodied in this myth of the centre-stone the result of the general direction of thought; as each people were certainly "the people" first born and best beloved of the gods, so their country occupied the centre of the world. It would be related how the oldest and most sacred city, or rather temple, was erected exactly on the navel. A story like this told of a temple would lead to the marking in the centre of its area the true middle point by a circular stone, a stone which would become most sacred and ceremonial in its import.'

And Dr. Schliemann thus writes of a central circle he unearthed in the palace at Tirynthus: 'In the exact centre of the hall, and therefore within the square enclosed by the four pillars, there is found in the floor a circle of about 3·30 m. diameter. There can be little doubt that this circle indicates the position of the hearth in the centre of the megaron. The hearth was in all antiquity the centre of the house, about which the family assembled, at which food was prepared, and where the guest received the place of honour. Hence it is frequently indicated by poets and philosophers as the navel or centre of the house. In the oldest time it was not only symbolically but actually the centre of the house, and especially of the megaron. It was only in later days, in the palaces of the great Romans, that it was removed from the chief rooms and established in a small by-room.'

All which may be true enough, and yet the placing of the hearthstone in the centre of the house may have had less reference to the earth-centre idea, than to the fact that in the circular huts of primitive man it was necessary to have a hole at the apex of the roof. Still, it is interesting to note that, as in the Imperial palace at Constantinople, so on the floor of St. Peter's at Rome, and elsewhere, is a flat circular slab of porphyry, associated with all ceremonials.

Is there any connection between the old central hearthstone and the Dillestein—Lid of Hell—one meets with in Grimm?

We have seen that the centre of the world is placed in Europe, in Asia, and in Africa, but who would expect to find it in America many centuries ago? Yet the traditions of Peru have it that Cuzco was founded by the gods, and that its name signifies 'navel'; and traditions of Mexico describe Yucatan as 'the centre and foundation' of both heaven and earth. We must, however, go back to the East as the most likely quarter in which to find it, and as the quarter to which the eyes of man have been most consistently turned.

To successive centuries of both Jews and Christians Jerusalem has been the centre of the world, and the Temple the centre of Jerusalem. The Talmud gives directions to those who are in foreign countries to pray with their faces towards the sacred land; to those in Palestine to pray with their faces towards Jerusalem; to those in Jerusalem to pray with their faces towards the Mount; to those in the Temple to pray with their faces towards the Holy of Holies. Now, this was not merely because this sacred spot was a ceremonial centre, but also because it was regarded as the geographical centre of the earth. According to the Rabbis the Temple was built on the great central rock of the world.

It is written in the Talmud: 'The world is like the eyeball of man: the white is the ocean that surrounds the wall, the black is the world itself, and the pupil is Jerusalem, and the image of the pupil is the Temple.' And again: 'The land of Israel is situated in the centre of the world, and Jerusalem in the centre of the land of Israel, and the Temple in the centre of Jerusalem, and the Holy of Holies in the centre of the Temple, and the foundation-stone on which the world was grounded is situated in front of the ark.' And once more: 'When the ark was removed a stone was there from the days of the first Prophets. It was called Foundation. It was three digits above the earth.'

This claim is direct enough, and at Jerusalem to this day in the Dome of the Rock, supposed to occupy the site of Solomon's Temple, is a bare stone which, as Sir Charles Warren was assured, rests on the top of a palm-tree, from the roots of which issue all the rivers of the world. The Mohammedans have accepted this same stone as the foundation-stone of the world, and they call it the Kibleh of Moses. It is said that Mahomet once intended making this the sacred centre of Islam, instead of Mecca, but changed his mind, and predicted that at the Last Day the black stone—the Kaabah—will leave Mecca and become the bride of the Foundation-stone at Jerusalem. So that there can be no possible doubt of the centre of sacred influences.

Concerning the stone at Jerusalem, Professor Palmer says: 'This Sakhrah is the centre of the world, and on the day of resurrection—it is supposed—the Angel Israfil will stand upon it to blow the last trumpet. It is also eighteen miles nearer heaven than any other place in the world, and beneath it is the source of every drop of sweet water that flows on the face of the earth. It is supposed to be suspended miraculously between heaven and earth. The effect upon the spectators, however, was so startling, that it was found necessary to place a building round it and conceal the marvel.'

According to Hittite and Semitic traditions mentioned by Professor Sayce and Professor Robertson Smith, there was a chasm in this central spot through which the waters of the Deluge escaped.

Right down to and through the Middle Ages Jerusalem was regarded by all Christians as the centre of the world; sometimes as the navel of the earth; and sometimes as the middlemost point of heaven and earth. The Hereford map of the thirteenth century, examined by Mr. Lethaby, shows the world as a plane circle surrounded by ocean, round whose borders are the eaters of men, and the one-eyed, and the half-men, and those whose heads do grow beneath their shoulders. 'Within this border we find everything the heart could desire; the sea is very red, the pillars of Hercules are pillars indeed; there is the Terrestrial Paradise enclosed by a battlemented wall, and unicorns, manticoras, salamanders, and other beasts of fascinating habits are clearly shown in the lands where they live. The centre of all is Jerusalem, a circular walled court, within which again is a smaller circle, the Church of the Holy Sepulchre.'

Even when the earth was recognised as a sphere, the idea of Jerusalem being the centre was not given up. Dante held to it, and veracious Sir John Mandeville endeavoured thus to explain away the difficulty: 'In going from Scotland or from England towards Jerusalem, men go always upwards, for our land is in the low part of the earth towards the west; and the land of Prester John is in the low part of the world towards the east; and they have the day when we have the night, and on the contrary they have the night when we have the day; for the earth and sea are of a round form, and as men go upward towards one point they go downward to another. Also you have heard me say that Jerusalem is in the middle of the world; and that may be proved and shown there by a spear which is fixed in the earth at the hour of midday, when it is equinoctial, which gives no shadow on any side.' Ingenious, if not convincing!

The Greek Church still regard Jerusalem as the middle of the world, and Mr. Curzon tells that in their portion of the Holy Sepulchre they have a magnificently decorated interior, in the centre of which is a globe of black marble on a pedestal, under which, they say, the head of Adam was found, and which they declare to be the exact centre of the globe.

The Mohammedans generally, however, regard the Kaabah at Mecca as—for the present, at any rate—the true centre. This stone is supposed to have been lowered directly from heaven, and all mosques are built to look towards it. Even in the modern schools of Cairo, according to Mr. Loftie, the children are taught that Mecca is the centre of the earth.

The Samaritans, however, look upon Gerizim as the holy mountain and centre of the religious and geographical world. And the Babylonians regarded the great Temple of Bel, according to Professor Sayce, as the house of the Foundation Stone of Heaven and Earth.

Gaya, again, is the Mecca of the Buddhists, where Buddha sat under the tree when he received enlightenment. This tree is the Bodhi tree described by Buddhist writers as surrounded by an enclosure rather of an oblong than of a square shape, but with four gates opening to the four cardinal points. In the middle of the enclosure is the diamond throne which a voice told Buddha he would find under a Pipal tree, which diamond throne is believed to be of the same age as the earth. 'It is the middle of the great Chiliocosm; it goes down to the limits of the golden wheel and upwards it is flush with the ground. It is composed of diamonds; in circuit it is a hundred paces or so. It is the place where the Buddhas attain the sacred path of Buddhahood. When the great earth is shaken this spot alone is unmoved. When the true law decays and dies it will be no longer visible.'

According to Sir Monier Williams, a stone marked with nine concentric circles is shown at Gaya as the diamond throne, and the Chiliocosm is not the centre of the world alone but of the Universe.

But in China, also a land of Buddhists, we find another centre, and in India there is an iron pillar at Delhi, dating from the fourth century, supposed by the Brahmans to mark the centre from their point of view. And in Southern India the Tamils have the Temple of Mandura, in the innermost sanctuary of which a rock comes through the floor, the roots of which are said to be in the centre of the earth.

The Indian Buddhists, of course, denied that China could be the Middle Kingdom, as the place where Buddha lived must necessarily be the centre. Nevertheless, the centre is now found by Chinese Buddhists in the Temple of Heaven at Pekin, where is one circular stone in the centre of circles of marble terraces, on which the Emperor kneels surrounded by circles—including that of the horizon—and believes himself to be in the Centre of the Universe and inferior only to Heaven.

But in the sixth century a certain Chinese traveller, called Sung-Yun, went to India for Buddhist studies, and he made his way by the Pamirs, the watershed of the great Asiatic rivers Indus and Oxus. And of this country he wrote:

'After entering the Tsung Ling mountains, step by step, we crept upwards for four days, and reached the highest point of the range. From this point as a centre, looking downwards, it seemed just as though we were poised in mid-air. Men say that this is the middle point of heaven and earth.'

This was written more than thirteen hundred years ago, and men to-day still call this part of Asia the Roof of the World.

Footnotes:

[1] Farrer: Primitive Manners.

[2] Lang: Custom and Myth.

[3] Lang.

[4] See Custom and Myth.

[5] In 'The Cruel Brother: A Tragedy.'

Milton Keynes UK
Ingram Content Group UK Ltd.
UKHW030909151124
451262UK00006B/870

9 789362 991942